Books by W. S. Merwin

POEMS

Opening the Hand   *1983*
Finding the Islands   *1982*
The Compass Flower   *1977*
The First Four Books of Poems   *1975*
(INCLUDING THE COMPLETE TEXTS OF
*A Mask for Janus, The Dancing Bears,
Green with Beasts* AND *The Drunk in the Furnace*)
Writings to an Unfinished Accompaniment   *1973*
The Carrier of Ladders   *1970*
The Lice   *1967*
The Moving Target   *1963*
The Drunk in the Furnace   *1960*
Green With Beasts   *1956*
The Dancing Bears   *1954*
A Mask for Janus   *1952*

PROSE

Unframed Originals   *1982*
Houses and Travellers   *1977*
The Miner's Pale Children   *1970*

TRANSLATIONS

From the Spanish Morning   *1984*
Four French Plays   *1984*
Selected Translations 1968–1978   *1979*
Osip Mandelstam, Selected Poems
(WITH CLARENCE BROWN)   *1974*
Asian Figures   *1973*
Transparence of the World (Poems by Jean Follain)   *1969*
Voices (Poems by Antonio Porchia)   *1969*
Products of the Perfected Civilization
(Selected Writings of Chamfort)   *1969*
Twenty Love Poems and a Song of Despair
(Poems by Pablo Neruda)   *1969*
Selected Translations 1948–1968   *1968*
The Song of Roland   *1963*
The Satires of Persius   *1960*
The Poem of the Cid   *1959*

Houses and Travellers

W. S. Merwin

HOUSES
AND
TRAVELLERS

Atheneum   New York

1984

The following appeared originally in THE NEW YORKER: The First Moon; The Taste; The Devil's Pig; The Element; The Great Union; A Fable of the Buyers; Speech of a Guide; The Chart; Chronicle; The Fugitive; The Crossroads; Port of Call; Path; Late Capital; By the Grain Elevators; The New World; A Voyage; The Ship from Costa Rica; The Old Boat; On the Map; Ten; A Parcel; The Ford; Wagon; A Street of Day; Watching a Train; The Field; Small Oak Place; Promontory; Harbor. Others appeared in the following magazines: Antaeus, The American Poetry Review, Chelsea, Lillabulero, Field, The Georgia Review, Seneca Review, Road Runner, Paris Review, Kayak, The Ohio Review, The Iowa Review, TriQuarterly, Mundus Artium, New American Review, Lotus, Goddard Journal, Leviathan, Tractor.

Library of Congress catalog card number 77-76474

ISBN 0-689-10817-6 (clothbound)

ISBN 0-689-70554-9 (paperback)

Published simultaneously in Canada by McClelland and Stewart Ltd

Manufactured by Halliday Lithograph Corporation,

West Hanover and Plympton, Massachusetts

Designed by Harry Ford

First paperback printing August 1977

Second printing January 1981

Third printing June 1984

FOR HARRY FORD

Contents

Contents

Houses and Travellers

The Nest

Apair of pigeons once discovered an open umbrella hanging by its handle from a beam, in an empty shed where a shepherd had left it. It was spring. They built their nest in the black web. The wind under the draughty roof rocked the umbrella, but nothing else disturbed them, nor their eggs, nor their firstborn.

The first pair of young learned to fly, and circled farther and farther over the countryside, and met with no mishap, until one day, when they were out by themselves, it rained. Between them and their home a dozen umbrellas opened. Suddenly it seemed to them that they were flying upside-down. They were terrified, as though they had learned all at once that they were on the wrong side of the light. They tried to fly on their backs, but they were dashed against the earth, where they were caught and eaten by the animals that were walking there all the time with their heads up, watching for something to fall.

The next pair of pigeons raised in the same nest met with the same fate, in the same way. And the next, and all the generations that followed. At last the parents grew too old to produce more young.

"Well," they said, "the nest won't be good much longer anyway." Over the years the accumulated crust of straw and droppings had rotted the fabric and it hung in tatters from the ribs.

"But not one of them ever came back," one of the parents said.

"That's natural, I suppose," the other answered. "They had to raise families of their own. This is the only nest here."

"Yes," said the first, "and they may have had to fly a long way to find another one like this."

EVERYTHING has its story. The story of the small black beetles, unable to fly, with a red bar on the upper half of each useless wing is that they are the soldiers of Pharaoh, still following the chosen people everywhere, with the Red Sea above their heads.

The story of the rough stone basin of the oldest fountain in the city is that it was once the oldest miser in the city, but the mercy of the world found him painful to look at, and changed him into a form which would permit him to say "I receive everything, I keep nothing," until he himself was completely worn away.

The story of the one-legged messenger is that his other leg is walking on the far side of death. "What seems to be over there?" they ask him. "Just emptiness?" "No," he says. "Something before that, with no name."

The story of the hinge is that it is learning to fly. "No hinge has ever flown," the locks tell it again and again. "That is why we are learning," it answers, "and then we will teach the doors."

Some things try to steal the stories of others. They have thieves' stories.

The story of each stone leads back to a mountain.

The locks say that it is possible for a thing to be separated from its story and never find it again in this world.

5

The First Moon

A PEBBLE is rolling along a road. It cannot see any-one. There is no one there to see it. So it rolls on. It cannot hear anyone. It rolls on all by itself under the sun. It thinks of the sun as one part of itself, some of the time, or—more exactly—as a feeling that recurs in one part of itself, hardly perceptible, at first, and then more intense, then much more intense, and then weaker and weaker until it is gone. While the feeling is there the pebble tries to carry as much of itself as possible into that part, dragging itself up from one side where it has become loose as though it had been uprooted. All of itself that it drags up on one side slides down the other, so as long as it feels the sun, the pebble rolls on and on, and it can feel itself moving faster, too, but it believes that its speed is the result of its growing lightness, which is caused by lifting more and more of itself off the ground.

All this time its shadow runs along under it like a friend trying to make it listen. And indeed the shadow is in constant fear, constant fear, striking against every ir-regularity in the road, knocked out of shape again and again, stretched, snatched at and caught by cracks and by all the bigger shadows along the way, and escaping from them all each time as though by miracle. "Stop, stop," it keeps calling. "Let us find somewhere of our own before night." The stone rolls on.

6

But it comes to roll more slowly. Not because it has listened to its shadow (it never listens) but because it has been thinking about a permanent place for the feeling of the sun. It has been considering turning into an eye. By the time it has decided, the day is over. The pebble rolls off the road into a wood, and stops. Its shadow falls asleep at once. The stone looks up. Clouds draw back. The eye opens. Night. Then deep in the stone the first moon rises.

The Broken

THE spiders started out to go with the wind on its pilgrimage. At that time they were honored among the invisibles—more sensitive than glass, lighter than water, purer than ice. Even the lightning spoke well of them, and it seemed as though they could go anywhere. But as they were travelling between cold and heat, cracks appeared in them, appeared in their limbs, and they stopped, it seemed they had to stop, had to leave the company of the wind for a while and stay in one place until they got better, moving carefully, hiding, trusting to nothing. It was not long before they gave up trying to become whole again, and instead undertook to mend the air. Neither life nor death, they said, would slip through it any more.

After that they were numbered among the dust—makers of ghosts.

The wind never missed them. There were still the clouds.

A N ant was born in an hourglass. Before it hatched out there was nothing to notice—and who would have looked, who would have suspected that one instant in each measure of time was an egg? And after the ant had emerged, it was too late to ask whether the birth was a mistake. Anyway, there was no one to ask, except those nameless hosts, his brothers, at once much older and much younger than he was, who nudged and ground past him, rustling toward the neck of the glass, and fell, and lay blind, deaf, and dreamless in the mountain made of each other, and would never hatch, though the mountain itself turned over again and again and sent them smoking down from its tip like souls into time. Besides, it never occurred to him that there was a question to ask. He did not know that things ever had been or ever could be any different, and whatever capacity for speech he may have been born with slept on inside him like a grain of sand.

There was nothing to eat. But he had never been told about hunger, and ants, particularly those of his species, can subsist for long periods, sometimes for generations, without consuming other life of any kind. The same was true of thirst, dry though that place surely was, made of nothing but those rocks his family. Whatever discomfort he may have become aware of, arising from either hunger or thirst, seemed to him to be like something that we would no doubt call a memory, returning inexplicably to trouble him in a new life, and certain to fade. It stirred in him like some ghost from his days as a grain of sand, but he could not remember what use it had been to him then. And he would hold it to him and save it for a while, as though there was a danger of losing it. He would hold it, trying to understand it, not knowing that it was pain. Something of the kind was true also of breathing. He was breathing. But he knew nothing of breath. What, after all, reached him through the glass? The light. The darkness. Sounds. Gravity. The desire to climb. What reached the grains of sand? Light. Darkness. Vibrations. Gravity. No one knows what else.

His brothers tried to crush him. He tried to count them. He could see that they were not infinite. But he could never start at the beginning. He would count them as they edged past him faster and faster. He had no names for numbers, but he tried to count the brothers even so, as he was borne along with them, as he climbed on their shoulders, as he swam on their heads, falling with them. He tried to count them as they fell on him and rolled after him to the foot of the next mountain, to the glass. He would start to the top again at once, trying to count them as they slipped under his feet. He would climb, counting, till the mountain turned over, and then he would begin again. Each time the mountain flowed out from under him he delayed the falling for an instant, and a measure of time paused while he clung to the neck of the glass, climbing on sand. Then everything went on just the same.

No one had told him about time. He did not know why he was trying to count. He did not know what a number, a final sum, would tell him, what use it would be to him, what he would call it, where he would put it. He did not know that they were not his real brothers. He thought he was a grain of sand.

He did not know that he was alone.

THE lonely child arranges all his toys in front of him.

"Come, play with me," he says to everyone who comes near. "Come and see all the toys I have."

But they go away.

So he smashes the first of the toys.

Then other children come to watch and help, and to fight over who can break his toys.

If a lonely child has no toys, he makes them.

The Salt Peddler

A MAN leading a horse was walking inland from the sea. The horse was loaded with sacks of salt which the man intended to sell in the city. It was summer and the salt peddler stopped to drink and to water his horse at every spring and stream he found on the way. When they had been travelling most of a day they came to a spring and stopped. The man drank, and then turned to draw the horse toward the water, but to his surprise the animal showed no sign of thirst, and refused. At this point the man noticed that one of the sacks had been torn or worn through, and that a thread of glittering white crystals was draining away onto the ground. The leak was so small as to be almost unnoticeable. On the other hand, it would be virtually impossible to mend it while the sack was full and on the horse's back. The man felt the sack to see whether much salt had been lost, and though it seemed to be as hard as ever, he traced the trail of salt a few steps back along the way he had come, wetting his fingers, touching the crystals he could see, putting the mixed salt and dust to the tip of his tongue, trying to guess how far back they led. When he looked up he saw that his horse had started to go on without him. Again the animal's behavior surprised him: the old horse had always been patient and dependable. He started after it, calling. Then he saw that there was a hand holding the reins, leading the horse. He could see the hand but nothing with it: no arm, no body, no garment. He continued to follow the horse, from a distance. And he stopped calling.

They went on in this way, uphill, downhill. Hours passed. The man had forgotten his thirst. He began to get used to his fear. He remembered the leak in the sack and began to worry about his load. He bent down to see whether he could still detect the trail of salt, and whether the salt was draining away faster or more slowly than before. There it was, visible here and there on the ground: a misty path of white crystals. No one else would have noticed it. He wet a finger again and touched the crystals and put the finger to his tongue and at the mixed taste of salt and dust he felt both anguish and relief.

When he looked up he saw that there was another man near him, also examining the dust of the path. The other man straightened, and their eyes met. They walked on together. It turned out that they were both going to the city. The other man did not at first say why he was going there, and the salt peddler felt ashamed to tell how he had allowed his horse to get away from him. They went forward in silence for a while. The salt peddler watched his horse, but as casually as he could. Finally he asked the other whether he was going to the city with something to sell. Yes, the other said. He explained that he was on his way there with a load of spices. He added, as though the salt peddler might not have heard of such things, that spices were worth more than their weight in gold. The salt peddler wanted to ask where the other man's load was, but before he had a chance to, the other man asked him whether he too was taking something to sell in the city. The peddler was ashamed to admit that the load with which he was travelling such a distance was nothing but plain salt. He answered that his wares consisted of precious stones. "Small precious stones," he added at once, deprecating them. "Mere dust of precious stones, in fact." As he said that, he felt that he was keeping closer to the truth. But even so, he explained, they too were worth far more than their weight in gold.

Then the two walked in silence for a while again, with the salt peddler stealing glances at the ground and at his horse, far ahead, with the hand still leading it. Finally the other man said that he had been wondering how much the small jewels and the jewel-dust were worth by the ounce, and whether the salt peddler would consider trading a certain quantity of jewel-dust for its value in spices. The salt peddler congratulated himself on having described his load as "mere dust of precious stones" —the phrase seemed to him even more honest than before. And he told himself that if he were a bit quick and a bit lucky, he should be able to trade some of his salt for spices worth more than their weight in gold, and get away before the other discovered the trick. The two started to bargain about the values of their respective wares. The salt peddler felt that he could afford to be generous, though not so generous as to excite suspicion. They agreed at last on terms that made the salt peddler's heart pound with anticipation. He asked where the load of spices was.

The other man sighed and said that when he had stopped, earlier in the day, for a drink of water, his horse had escaped from him and was by now some distance ahead. The salt peddler looked ahead but saw only his own horse, and a large bank of cloud or mist lying across the path, into which his horse disappeared as he watched. The path could be seen emerging again on the other side of the cloud, but the disappearance of the horse troubled him, and he quickened his steps.

"Where is your load?" the other asked him, keeping up with him.

He explained that his horse too had escaped, and that he had just lost sight of it.

"I can't see mine any longer, either," the other man said.

They hurried on to the bank of cloud. The salt peddler shivered, and stepped in. It was cold inside the cloud, and dark like a winter day, and there was a sound of rushing water. The peddler heard his companion's footsteps and breath beside him. He felt the cloud condense on his face and run down into his clothes. He worried about the salt in the sacks.

At last he and the other man came to the edge of a small cliff above a stream. Down beside the water he saw his horse.

"There he is!" the salt peddler said.

"I see mine too," the other said.

"There's only one horse that I can see," the peddler said.

"It's true. I see only one," the other answered.

"Well, that one's my horse," the salt peddler said, raising his voice.

"He's mine!" the other answered, laughing, but raising his voice too. And they both slipped and scrambled down the steep slope toward the stream. The hand was still leading the horse, and kept it well ahead of them. They followed it along the water. After they had gone a little way, the salt peddler saw, to his distress, that the horse was being led across the stream, going in deeper at every step. The animal sank to its shoulders and began to swim. The peddler groaned to think of the remaining salt in the sacks. He wondered whether any would be left at all. He and the other man plunged into the stream and floundered through the salty water. On the other side, the horse led them on toward a figure sitting in the mist farther up the stream. As they drew nearer, the salt peddler saw that it was an old man, with what appeared to be water running from one hand. The other hand was missing. Then the peddler saw the hand that was leading the horse go up to the old man's wrist and join it, and the old man looked up.

"Welcome," he said. "Is this your horse?"

"Yes," the salt peddler said.

"Yes," the other man said.

"Where were you going with it?" the old man asked.

And they both told him that they were on their way to the city. The old man looked at them both, then at one, then at the other.

"Long ago," he said, "two brothers set out to found that city. Before they began it, one brother killed the other. I was the one who was killed. There is my city, beyond me."

The peddler looked past him and saw a forest of towers and spires gleaming with bright metals and jewels.

"My brother has not been seen for centuries in his city," the old man continued, "but I have never left mine. And yet I cannot say that I am happy here. No one is happy here. I was never able to forget the life that I had hoped to go on with. Age after age I cherished the hope that I might do something for the living. Finally I was granted the task of making tears."

He held up his left hand, from which the drops continued to fall.

"I thought that the labor would make me happy, or at least resigned," he said, "but here, at least, what is given with one hand is taken away with the other. The tears that I made were tasteless. Up until that time people had wept, as they had done everything else, with ease of heart. Weeping was a pleasure like any other. But once their tears came from me, their weeping was insipid, and those who wept were condemned to supply the saver themselves, to which end grief and bitterness were born. After that, even when people wept for joy their joy contained the reminder and the taste of anguish. But I have not been able to forget the time when it was not so, and I long, age after age, to obtain salt, to spare them their pain. I know it is still there, I call out to it, I send my own hand away into the world to try to lead it to me. I would give anything for it. What were you taking to the other city?"

"Salt," the other man answered.

"Then the horse must be yours," the old man said. "But the salt itself never reaches me. Just the same, if you wish to, you may fill the sacks with jewels."

He held out the reins to the other man.

"But the horse is mine!" the salt peddler said.

"Your horse was already loaded with jewels," the other man said, and took the reins.

"He's mine, he's mine!" the salt peddler shouted, and he picked up a large stone and struck the other on the head, and saw him fall.

"Now he can stay here," the old man said. "You may as well take his horse." And the salt peddler felt the reins in his hand once more, and felt his eyes fill with tears so that he could see nothing, and he fell to his knees beside the body, and sobbed. When he wiped his eyes and looked up again there was no one else to be seen. The city had disappeared. The cloud was blowing away. And he stood up and turned the horse's head and started back toward the sea with his empty sacks.

The Water Clock

I T is said that the first victim who fell to the armed men as they emerged from the wooden horse on the last night of Troy was a young man leaning over the stone lip of a water clock in the city square. There had long been a legend among the inhabitants that the city would never fall without being warned by the water clock. The young man was the hereditary keeper of the clock, and came to visit it at the end of each watch. As he crossed the square that night he thought he heard a hollow sound coming from the horse. He stopped in the middle of the square and waited, and then he heard the same sound—and recognized it—coming from his own heart. At the same time he heard the water clock whispering, and he went to it, and set his torch in a socket, and leaned over the rim. He saw—as he had seen all his life—the carved faces on the stone buckets, and their reflections in each of the surfaces of the water, forming a series that included the reflection of his own face, and went on, upwards and downwards, until it passed out of sight, and each of the dripping stone faces, and its reflection, was whispering, "Listen, listen, listen." So he listened, and heard the echo of his own heart, and within it the echo of feet running. Then the spear found him.

When the survivors of Troy built their city, they too set a water clock in the main square, and modelled it as closely as they could on the one they remembered, but they no longer believed in the legend.

The Taste

THERE is a drink which only the old ever taste. Everyone knows that the day is full of rocks, some large, some small, which move. They are all invisible and no one mentions them, but everyone knows that they are rocks. No one knows how to get past them, or to enter them, or to see what is inside them. They are said to contain the treasure of Age, which no one has ever looked on—a black treasure.

At night when only the old are awake, black springs rise in some of the rocks and begin to flow toward some of the old. The slow streams seldom choose for destinations the old who are nearest to them. The rocks in which they rise have all moved. The withered body toward which a stream starts to make its way may have passed the source years before and not have known it. How wide the world is now! How empty! How far a stream may have to flow! Meanwhile the old are dying.

As a stream passes through the dark meadows, birds that are standing there turn to look. Each time they think it is Memory once more. But it is not Memory. Each of the birds was a color, once, and this is where they go.

When at last a stream lies on the tongue it set out for, it rests. There is a moment of trembling. Tears come out and sit in the night. After a while the stream gets up and goes to its boat and loads the old person into it and they drift away together toward the valley. In the morning the body that has been visited can no longer stand, no longer speak. It swallows and swallows as though trying to remember tasting water for the first time.

A Conversation

THERE is a wind that when it turns I hear the garden
and the desert discussing things with each other.
Sometimes in the garden, sometimes in the desert, day
or night. Mud walls, stone walls, no walls, limestone,
sheep far away, howling, birds singing, hissing, trickling,
silence, dry smells, watered smells, moons, stars, flowers
that are keys between them.

They tell their dreams to each other, the garden and
the desert. They dream above all of each other. The
desert dreams of the garden inside it. It loves the garden.
It embraces the garden. It wants to turn it into desert.
The garden lives within itself. It dreams of the desert
all around it, and of its difference from the desert, which
it knows is as frail as feeling.

It must be a long time since I first heard them talking.
I must have heard them when I was two. I must have
heard them when I was one, and so on. Perhaps before
I was born. Or anyone was born. Or any roundness be-
came an egg. Or the water was born, cooling on a high
rock, prophesying tears, prophesying eyes.

I must have heard them even before the rocks were
born moving in the colored night. Probably I have heard
them ever since the light began looking for something to
write on, flying on, white, with the colors hidden inside
it and the darkness around it, forgetting nothing from

the beginning, prophesying the end of knowledge, prophesying the wilderness, prophesying the garden, prophesying the wilderness dreaming that it was a garden. And the garden. And the wilderness.

The River of Fires

F AR in the north, where trees are thin and scarce, there is a wide river along whose banks every hour a fire is lighted farther upstream. This happens in the summer, when the days never end, and the smoke rises from fire after invisible fire, all the way out to the sky. And in the winter, when the blazing points can often be seen for great distances, as though the sky were beginning to flatten out, and new planets were set in it, glowing red because they were rising horizontally; and then whoever looks, sooner or later is overtaken with a sense of being the darkness fleeing before them. It happens in the fogs in the spring and fall, when even fires cannot be seen at a slight distance, and then suddenly they emerge in a gleaming cloud. And so time is constantly moving upstream. As it must, they feel in that country, if they are to live. And on the last night of the year the last fire is allowed to go out, by a clear stream in the mountains to the south, and on the first morning of the year, in the minutes after midnight, a fire is lit on the ice where the river flows into the frozen sea, on the west bank, and is carried across the river-mouth to the east bank and there built higher and higher, into a vast and desperate steaming conflagration, to help the sun to rise through the ice. And then hour by hour they go ahead, guiding him up the river under the ice, until he rises at last, and then until he never sets, and until after he has gone. They never reach the source. They believe that they would drown, or be frozen into the glacier, still facing south, like some of the heroes of their legends. They bury their dead beyond the last ashes, where the river is always cold and no one has ever explored the mountains.

A GIRL is walking down the thousands of winding steps in front of the palace, carrying a bucket of water. The long pink light flicks open and shut between her feet.

Meanwhile a herd of horses is massed at the eastern gate, which appears to be open. Beyond the gate is the night without stars. Those horses have been captured again and again, and have escaped again and again, after each battle, leaving their riders dead on the field, and have found their way to the gate looking for their true master, from whose black meadow they were stolen, unbroken.

Each of the horses is a drop of water in the bucket she is carrying. Whenever a little bit splashes onto the stairs or onto her feet, a knot of horses plunges through the gate and is swallowed up in the darkness as in sand.

The life of each horse is an eon of sunlight. As each horse vanishes, the death of the sun moves millions of years closer to us. She is carrying in that bucket the whole age of the sun, from the beginning, from long before us, when there was only the black meadow and the silent fountain. If the bucket were to fall, nothing would ever have been.

The horses are crowded against the open gateway. Far below her there is a single tree dying of drought.

But her eyes are not on the tree, nor on the stairs, nor on anything in front of her. She is thinking of her lover, whom she has never seen because he comes to her only by dark.

THE harvest was over. Even the scythe had not been mine. I had nowhere to go.

In the evening I found a young woman lying on the ground like a sheaf of wheat, radiant and silent. When I bent over her she was watching me, smiling.

I carried her into an empty house among the trees. Next to the kitchen there was a room with a bed and a colored quilt. I put her there and stood between two sources of light, and the room was brighter than the day outside.

She is helpless. She cannot speak. I will take care of her.

It is her house. I learned that from a woman who came to the door almost at once, and called to her, and tried to trick me, charm me, frighten me, get rid of me. Old and poisonous. When at last she went away, she left, under the bushes by the house, a rabbit from the mown fields, that pretends to be dead, to be half-skinned, to have no eyelids, so that it can watch what I do.

It has watched me before. I will not leave.

When I shut my eyes I see the wheat.

The Bride of the East

A GIRL fell in love with the East and said she would marry no other. When her father heard of this he went to talk with her. He described to her all the kingdoms of the earth. He told her of the pleasures of the south, he was eloquent in praise of the glories of the north, he lifted a corner of the horizon to let her catch a single glimpse of the west. But she would not look and would not listen.

"Why the East?" her father said.

"Everything comes from him," she answered.

"But the East cannot marry you," her father said, as gently as he could. She sat still, at the window.

"The East cannot even come to you," her father went on.

"He can," she said.

"You would not be here," her father said. "You would be far away, to the west of here."

"He would see me," she answered.

"Even if you were still visible you would be too far to recognize: a very small black figure sitting in a frame full of darkness, travelling backwards into a mountain."

"I will not have gone," she said. "I will have waited."

"You can't wait," he answered.

"Why not?"

"Even now you're going."

"It's not true."

"Each time you sleep you wake up farther away."

"Farther from where?"

"From here."

"I don't care."

"Farther from the East."

"I've stopped sleeping." And it was true. Ever since she had fallen in love she had sat awake all night, every night, looking out of the east window.

"Each time you blink your eyes, when you open them you are farther."

"Only from here," she said.

"From the East," he insisted.

"No," she said. "He can go faster."

"Nothing is faster than you when you close your eyes."

"He'd be there."

"He wouldn't stay."

"And I've stopped closing them." It was true. As she sat looking out of the window, her eyes never blinked, day or night.

"I want you to go to sleep now, and tomorrow we can talk about other things," her father said.

"I don't want to sleep," she said. "You just don't want me to marry the East. Why don't you want me to marry the East?"

"I want you to marry someone from here."

"I don't want anybody from here."

"You will."

"I can't even see them. I look at their faces and all I see is holes."

"That's because your head is full of the East. But it will be different in the morning, you'll see."

"Besides, I've stopped looking at them." It was true. All she looked at now was the sky beyond the frame of the window facing east, which was then growing dark.

"I suppose that when you look at my face you see nothing but a hole too," he said. It was a trick to make her turn and look at him, but she was used to his tricks, and never took her eyes from the window. "But we're all becoming that way. You too," he said. "We're fading away so that we can't be seen at all. We're beginning to look just like air, so that even if he could come here he wouldn't be able to find you."

It was another trick to make her look, but she knew it.

"He's already found me," she said. At this her father was startled, for a moment. Then he grew angry, which is not always an aid to illumination.

"I don't believe you," he said—harshly, because it was not wholly true.

"And you will never marry him," he added, with deliberate cruelty.

"I'm already his bride," she said.

This made her father still more angry.

"It's impossible," he insisted. But nothing would change her thoughts nor turn her gaze from the window.

"Very well," her father said. "Wait for him." And he sent for men to brick up the east window. But she was still there the next morning. And the next evening, and the following morning. She was still there when the bells rang for Sunday, and she was still there when they rang for Easter. She was still there when they rang for her brother's wedding and when they tolled for her mother's passing, and when they rang for her father's burial, and for her brother's death, and others' deaths, and fires in the city, and storms in summer, and sieges and victories and griefs, and when the walls fell behind her because the place had stood uninhabited and untended for so long, the roof letting in until the beams rotted and then moss rooted along them and led the way down and the light followed and she was still there sitting by the bricked-up east window from which not a single brick had fallen, because scar tissue holds longer than the original. But she noticed nothing until they took down the east wall too, finally, because it was unsafe, and because they wanted the stones from the window-frame, and the space in which to put something else, and then of course the bricks fell at her feet, and she stood up and held out her hands toward the east, and feeling nothing there, took a stop forward.

It is one of her withered hands that you feel occasionally on your arm, a second at a time, in an episode that must surely last for more than one life. Often it is dark when her finger touches you, and so you may not at first notice that she is blind, and is groping with both hands in one direction. She is looking for the brick wall beyond which is the East, whose image is still in her breast, but the bricks have gone, and while they were there she had lost her ability to see anything except the darkness of the east, which looks like other darkness. But once she touches you she seems to know where she is going, and she leads you through the dark tree-lined square to an unlit doorway. It appears to you that there is a scorpion on one side of the doorway and a worm on the other side. They are bowing to each other, but straighten as you approach, and are heard saying to each other, as you pass through,

"My old friend." (This is the scorpion.)

"My very old friend." (This is the worm, answering.)

"I never wanted bones."

"Neither did I." (The worm again.)

"I'm better off without them."

"That's what I say to myself. If I say anything."

"You should consider having eyes, though."

"What would I want with eyes?"

"You'd see."

"Who needs to see?"

"The bride of the East."

"What for? Only the East can pass through this door and live."

But you are not the East. You are subject to every wind that blows. And as you turn to tell her, she is not there.

The Footstep

NOON, then, is the name of the ninth angel, where he falls, where he was always going to fall, where he plummets into our world as surely and as regularly as the sun rises. Outside the books and the histories, the name was always going to mean no one, none, nothing.

And the world knows it. Everywhere it can tell that he is coming, that he is falling. The animals move into the shade of trees, and watch, hardly breathing. The birds find a little darkness, and pause. A film like dust veils the shining leaves. In the unlit hives the bees dance more slowly and come to a stop. Silence leaks into the dreams of the bats. The breeze dies. You shiver. He strikes. He is there.

At that point in time and space all directions are burned away. Where he touches, there is no promise of continuing, no reason nor direction to follow—or so it seems. But he is also one of the angels of turning, and we turn, and the air springs up again, and the day goes on, leaving behind it one more empty footstep, the place and the mark of no one.

Even among the waves, every ninth one is his, and when it reaches the shore those that follow it recede.

You know that he is one of the seals of death. But you can see, too, if your eyes can bear it, that he is an angel,

33

one of the falling angels, who in his splendor aspires to rule heaven himself—which is why he falls. Some go so far as to insist that his beauty exceeds that of all the sons of morning.

August

I<small>N</small> August many, even of those who will not leave, turn idle, seek out each others' company, and rove together in restless bands, aimlessly but impatiently, as though somewhere else a place were being made ready for them. Voices of things unattached, of shutters, of dead ivy, and the nesting warnings of birds, go on because they forget to stop. Bells feel their age. There is gray in the grass, and the verbs stand still at unmarked crossroads.

In August names dangle, more or less, the wheat rattles, its time has come, plums prepare to fall, hands go out by themselves, far from the heart and the spring. It is hard to remember any of these days later. If ever one reappears it is without a shape of its own—a phase of an interval, a face bending over a dry pond.

In August even the cries urging dogs to bring in the cows meet and fly together, circling higher and higher in the evening sky, and a widow forgets everything and runs out calling a dog that has been dead for years. The coolness after sudden showers already belongs to autumn, although the water in the stone basins is still warm as blood. Loosestrife, and the acanthus stained with mourning. Few things are begun, lest they be overtaken.

In August the rumors grow into hay. It is a time that has been given many gods, but none of them stayed, and none returned. It was named at last for an emperor who they pretended was one of the immortals, who ruled an empire which they pretended was eternal, its provinces the colors of straw, sand, dry leaves. An empire the color of honey, without the taste. A realm of yellow glass. It too was named for him, and they called it Peace, and his, and they said it was the whole of the world, and that beyond it there was nothing but darkness. But even at the time there were gossip-mongers who insisted that they remembered him for whom it was all named, shaken with a fit of rage in the very doors of the senate, seizing a senator, and with his own fingers tearing out both of the man's eyes.

The Fly and the Milk

A FLY may be waiting for the milk every day. The milk changes but it's the same fly.

The milk that the fly has drunk turns into the same fly, and from then on it stays the same, while the rest of the milk goes on changing.

So one hand puts a big white stone in the milk place.

The fly wants to fly away after stopping to drink white stone, but it isn't a fly any more. It doesn't have the soul of a fly. It's a stone with no color. A small dry stone in a desert, from then on, with sand children. Children that are not even real children. Even when they fall into milk they don't know it.

From then on there is no fly, and the milk stays the same.

THE devil's pig cannot be killed. And you too are happy to hear it—quite as happy as anyone else. Not because pigs are the most intelligent of domestic animals. Is intelligence grounds for mercy? Humans have never been certain that it is not in itself a crime. Yet they feel obligated to it, they depend on it, and so they pass laws declaring that it is a virtue. But they are still hungry. And pigs in numbers like the stars of heaven have not been fattened for their virtue but for their flesh: to bleed at the eyes, to wear the blue rind and the colorless wounds, never to know age, but to fill with the jellied waters of silence, and be sundered and pass, fiber by fiber, through the mouths of humans. But not the devil's pig.

Of course he is beautiful. He is reared by a family who become fond of him, and display him to visitors, and the children scratch him and ride him, and everyone says it is a pity, and when the time comes and he is held down, and the neighbor who always does the job holds the knife at the stretched throat and pushes, suddenly the neighbor is kneeling at the edge of a kite, with a glue-brush in his hand, trying to mend a gash that he himself has made, while everyone watches in silence, for it is a kite that everyone in the village loved. And the neighbor works for a long time, without a word, while the family stands over him, and at the end he bends forward and breathes on the patched place to make it whole, and then stands and gives the mended kite to the children, and goes home afterward as though he had been to a funeral all by himself.

Sometimes the devil's pig takes all the prizes and is the sire of a famous progeny, and a center of envy and scheming, and is stolen, and is the pretext for murder and imprisonment and despair, and is returned to his owner, and survives him, and they say he will be allowed to die of old age, but before the first sign of it he disappears, and after that no one in that part of the country trusts anyone else, day or night, for generations.

He lives with a saint and is a model of obedience, and tramples on snakes, and is given away, but never forgotten.

He rides in the truck with the others, and climbs the ramp with them, and at the top the man with the stunner sees the little dog from home running up the ramp with the pigs, and the man shuts the gate and stops the braid of backs, and picks up the little dog and takes him out and sends him home with a pat and never sees him again.

Can you imagine killing him? Can you envisage what it would do to you? Can you think how the devil would treat you after that—your sleep, what you would hear at table, who would pray with your lips? But you do not wish to kill the devil's pig.

He has become the pride of the emperor, and his statute has been carved, and armies, after victories, have the right to carry his image on a banner. He fears neither fire nor water. He loves everyone. Why should he not? His master is the lord of this world.

Iron

I n the age of iron they learned to make filings. They were led to the lodestone and their names for it drifted closer to the words for loving, but were never the same. They discovered how to induce the lodestone to impart its paradoxical virtues to the shoe of a horse, and they taught themselves how to make paper, and make it white. Onto the lodestone-inspired shoe of an unseen horse, in time they laid an empty white leaf of paper and onto the paper they threw the filings they themselves had made, and what they saw then was the rose of the world, with its two eyes and two hearts. One day they set it adrift in a boat, and the iron rose of the world went sailing, the whole world following after. But its north always varied from the true north, and in itself it was never sure by how much.

The horseshoe was made for holding the virtues of the lodestone long before the first horse was domesticated, and from having the horseshoe they conceived of having the horse. Generations of blacksmiths died in ignorance of the drift of their destiny, before the first of them was led to the lodestone. But the horse for which the first horseshoe was made is still unbroken. From the very beginning you could hang up the sacred horseshoe from a tree and strike it once anywhere with an iron stick and all its virtue would fly out of it in a single cascading

bird-note, one beat of the galloping horse, after which
it will lie still on the ground and let the filings rest over
it evenly like dust or snow, itself still nailed to the horse's
footprint. And you could do it all again.

They made a drawing of the rose and laid the horse-
shoe at the edge of it and set them adrift, and the picture
sailed away with the horse at its prow, and its tiers of oar-
less petals, but its north was not the true north, in the
sky. Instead, its north turned in varying circles, wander-
ing through infinite outer worlds, at inconceivable dis-
tances from the still beam at its true center. How long
ago it began! Before the first blacksmith was born, whales
sleeping in calm water would swing slowly to face north,
the position in which they gave birth. The north of the
horse, and of iron, and of iron's rose. The north of the
file and of blood, and of ambition and the amber of com-
merce. Not the axis close beside it, turning in each of
them.

He Who Made the Houses

H E was a man whose age nobody knew, and no-
body could remember what he did before. All
that time he had lived alone. He had lived simply. He
looked like wax, but somewhere he was burning. He was
always bent at his labor, even when he seemed to be
looking at you. His eyes were always on his love, which
was the work of his life. He made all kinds of houses,
complete with the tools, habits, passages, hiding places,
traps, cupboards, pictures, furry corridors, ice chimneys,
rotted stairs, laid tables, smells, and bone-filled dens, of
lives. Out of everything he could find, beg, borrow, or
take away until he could try it first, he made these houses,
of all sizes, opening onto every prospect, or dug into the
ground. Everywhere that he could persuade someone
to let him use the space and let him alone there for a
while, he made those houses. He made them on some
of the oldest, and on some of the poorest places, and on
many others.

At least once a year—he would explain, when you
could get him to answer you—all the words fly up from
the places where they have been discontented. For a
moment so small that you do not notice it, they leave
their comfortless and insecure lodgings altogether, and
fly through the air like a swarm of bees. Some people
can hear them. He, for instance, could hear them. During

those moments which even to him seemed indescribably short, the words manage to travel great distances. Each time it happens that some of them never get back, or end up in other places and nobody knows it, and after that, more people do not understand something, many things, each other, themselves, or all of these, and they believe that they and what they do not understand are being represented by the same words, when they are not even using words that live in the same places any more.

But if each of the words had the house that was right for it, it would go on living there, or if it did go away for a while it would want to come back to the same place. He had always suspected this, and had discovered that it was in fact so, because he had made a study of words, and ever since then he had been making houses for each one of them. Because he knew their ways he could describe how they would come, on a certain day, like bees indeed, like bees, closer and closer, having caught a glimpse of their true homes.

"Are they all like insects, then?" you might ask.

"You know they are not," he would answer. "Some are like shrews, some are like birds, some are like water, or friends of various kinds, some are like old aunts, some are like lights, some are like feet walking without bodies in a hall lined with everything any of us remembers, and so forth. They are like us. Each of them has to have been offered its rightful abode if we are to be able to speak from one day to the next and know what we mean."

He was far advanced in his task when the barbarians arrived with their axes.

HE had told the young woman about the old man, his hero, who had taught him more than anyone else. A man of great reserve, absolute independence, integrity, lucidity, charity, calm, and genius, living alone after a life of attachments. It is always hard to meet a hero again, nevertheless the young man had been happy when he, the young woman, and the old man were invited to the same gathering at a place in the country. It was at the edge of a little village with stone houses. The light was green and rainy.

But they were there for several days, and after a while he began to feel that they would never get away from the old man—not so old now as he remembered him—who seemed to be everywhere, sat with them at table, and talked and talked, always brilliantly, marvellously, quietly. The younger man watched him grow shorter, and broader, and pinker, and limper. Then he imagined, with intricate disappointment, that the older man was attracted to the young woman.

He and she went out after lunch; he hurried her out right after the coffee, in nothing but her white dress, although it was raining a little. She was very patient. They walked in the lane. It wasn't raining hard. It was warm. She asked him why he was in a hurry. He said, "To get away from him for a little," and he laughed.

44

But she didn't. So then he was more serious, a little irritated with her too, saying that the man was becoming excessive, and she urged him to be patient, which annoyed him. There was a well in the middle of the lane, with an arch of black iron over it, from which a bucket hung, and as they were walking around it he saw that the older man was following them.

He said to her, "Don't look now, he's following us."

"Maybe not," she said.

"Yes, he is," he said. "He's by himself."

"Oh," she said.

He said, "If we don't catch his eye, maybe he'll turn back."

"Don't do that," she said.

"Yes," he said. "I want some time to ourselves," he said. He saw that the older man was waving, but pretended not to see. He thought of the older man watching him lead her out through the rain, and perhaps wondering whether he was taking proper care of her, she looked so young, and coming along to be protective in some way. Holding hands, he led her along to a stone tower on the lane, that was part of the grounds, an annex of the main house. He drew her into the tower, as though to get out of the rain.

"No, don't do that," she said. "Be kind to him."

When he was safely in the dark he looked back, and the older man was at the well. "Let's go upstairs," he said, knowing the place. "We can't not have seen him and then seem to be waiting for him." She agreed, and they went up. The tower room was furnished as it had always been. They sat on the bed. They weren't very wet. They weren't cold. They were listening. They were even laughing a little.

"He's coming," she said.

He said, "Be quiet."

"If he comes in we'll have to call to him," she said.

45

"He'll know we can hear him, and if we don't call we'll seem to be hiding."

"He doesn't know that we know who it is," he said.

"What if he comes up and finds us," she said.

"He won't want to come up the stairs," he said. "He'll understand that we want to be by ourselves."

"No," she said, "I don't want him to think we're hiding from him."

They said nothing for a while, and listened. A long time, sitting on the foot of the bed.

"He's not coming," she said. Then they heard him, scraping his feet on the stones outside.

"If he comes in, I'll go out and look down," she said.

"No, I will," he said. They heard the older man step inside, and the young man went out and looked down and said, "Oh hello."

"I brought something to show you," the older man said, after a moment of just standing there looking up. "This is as good a place as any," he added.

From above, he looked still shorter and pinker, with the wet head much larger than the rest of him, and the face hanging in folds. He turned to the stairs and started up slowly, and the younger man had to stand and watch, and apologize for having brought him out in the rain, while the older man said nothing, all the way up the stairs, and seemed to be in no hurry. He went through the door first, and then they all three stood facing each other, saying nothing, and gave a little laugh together.

Then the older man started to talk, and talked about lunch, and afterthoughts, and then he said he had something to show the younger man—to show to them both. He said he wanted to show these things to someone, after all, and it sounded as though he had never shown them to anyone. He asked their permission. He drew from under his coat a folder and laid it on the four-poster bed, and began to spread out drawings and paintings that he had done. Some of them were in white on black or dark colored paper, but most of them were in color. In the colored ones the sky was invariably a solid blue, the earth was almost always a uniform shade of tan, and on the tan earth pieces of architecture stood in monolithic isolation, some of them with a single window, with a face in it. Perfect curves, in black, connected the tops of the buildings with each other, and on each black line, or path, like a single bead, was a planet, in which a landscape appeared, rising through a face. The white paintings on dark paper depicted animals, in such a way that their shapes looked like skeletons of further bodies.

She made a few exclamations, but the older man seemed to pay no attention. The younger man said they were very powerful. There were little poems written on some of them, a few lines each. He bent to read the poems in their small careful script, and later could not remember any. He repeated the few things he had said before. And he said he knew someone who would be interested in seeing them.

Then the older man said that he imagined they would like to be by themselves for a bit, and he gathered up the paintings deliberately, and seemed about to give them to the younger man, but didn't. They all three started down the stairs together, with the older man herding them in front. At the bottom of the stairs the older man insisted on going back alone the way he had come, while they continued their walk, since it had stopped raining. They left by another door, and the young man did not want to look at her at all.

L YING on the floor of the veranda, in the dark, he considered the fact that he had never in his life been so far off the ground. He had known it would be so today, but he had not thought about it that way. He had not thought about it in so many words. The fourth floor. At each floor, on the way up, he had seen a double door without a handle, that looked like a sliding lid. Each double door had a sign over it saying "Elevator," and on the door there was an orange paper pasted, on which the same hand had printed the words "Out of Order." He had seen all that in the daylight, in the early afternoon, as he had climbed.

He had wondered what time to come. The professor's note from the capital had said simply to come on the ninth. Why don't you come on the ninth. Why don't you come on the ninth. That was all it said, and he had tried to extract more information, just from the wording, but without success. It was written on university stationery, with a city address. He had never been to the city, but now was the time. He knew the day but not the hour. So he planned to arrive in the morning.

He took the night train, which got you into the city in the early hours when the sky was just growing light and the carts and trucks were rolling through the out-skirts, converging on the market place, the wet stones, the waiting cats. He could see the cats in the first gray light as the train entered the station, where everybody got off and became a crowd, hurrying definitely, mingling with other hurrying streams of people. Inside the station they began to swirl and go off in different directions, and the current dissipated itself, died out at counters where tickets, food, or magazines were for sale. The sound of feet everywhere. The people standing in backwaters were closed in on themselves, busy thinking of tickets, or else eating, or buying or counting money, not looking at him drifting among them. He asked a small old man in a dark suit the way to the university, but the old man stared at him and did not answer. He asked a heavy man in a cap with a polished black visor, who said, "Out there," and pointed, and walked away.

He went out through the door the man had pointed to. The noise of the city struck him in waves. A woman selling fruit told him what street to follow. She said it was a long way.

It was a few miles, through the sound of traffic. But the day was Saturday, and almost no one was at the university. The doors seemed to be locked. A young man with a bicycle told him how to find the architecture building. The glass doors at the front would not open, and no one came when he knocked, but a smaller door, on the side, opened when he pulled it, and he went in and walked along the reverberating marble halls until a man in a uniform appeared around a corner and asked what he wanted.

When he said he wanted to see the professor, the man was unwelcoming. Said it was not possible to see the professor. The professor wasn't there.

The young man asked him if he knew the professor, and the man said of course he did. He said he was the superintendent of the building. "Today's Saturday," he said.

"Yes," the young man said.

"And anyway, you need an appointment," the man said. "Not just anybody can walk in." He stepped forward and took the young man by the arm.

The young man said that the professor had told him to come.

"What for?"

"To see him."

"What about?"

"I wrote him a letter."

"You can't just go walking around through the building," the superintendent said, and began to turn him around.

"He told me to come," the young man repeated.

"Not today," the superintendent said.

"Yes, today," the young man said. "The ninth."

"Come along," the superintendent said.

"The ninth," the young man said again.

"Didn't you hear me, today's Saturday," the superintendent said. "He's never here on Saturday, unless it's to work, and then he won't see anybody."

"But he said today," the young man said.

"He isn't here," the superintendent said, growing taller as he said it, and pleased.

The young man dug the letter out of an inside pocket, and said, "Look. 'Why don't you come on the ninth.' " He read the words out distinctly, pointing at each one with his finger. Then there was a pause.

"That's different," the superintendent said. He passed his fingers over his head as though he had just lifted a hat off, and said, "That's for the party, of course." He patted the young man on the shoulder. "But that's not here."

"Where is it?"

"It's not now, either. It's later on."

"Where will it be?"

"Some of the students are giving it."

"Where?"

"You'd never find them," the superintendent said. "I know they had a number of things planned. But they were all for later on."

"But where?"

"Then they were going back to his place afterward. The way they always do," the superintendent said, and he was glad to show he knew it.

"I'll go there, then," the young man said.

"Not now," the superintendent said.

"When?"

"I'll call up his apartment house," the superintendent said. "Wait here." And he went off down the hall and left the young man standing there. When he came back he said that in the professor's building they did not know the professor's plans.

"Can't you telephone to him?" the young man asked.

"No, no. Can't do that. But I know you can't go out there in the morning. I know that."

And the superintendent told the young man the address and how to get there, in exchange for a promise not to go until the afternoon. He did not say what time in the afternoon, and the young man thought about it as he went. The streets grew quieter.

The address was in a neighborhood of buildings several storeys high, all of which the professor and his students had designed, so the superintendent had told him. There were courtyards between them, with flowerbeds enclosed by low walls. It was a sunny afternoon. He felt too warm in his long overcoat, which was never warm enough when he wore it on Sundays, at home in the country. He found the entry. He waited until he heard two o'clock strike, and then he rang the downstairs bell, but nothing happened. He opened the door and went to the elevator, read the orange paper, and started to climb the stairs. Each flight turned on itself, and at the top gave onto a wide, long veranda overlooking the courtyard. An apartment door opened off each veranda. Benches, ivy gardens furnished the verandas, and flowers were planted along the balustrades. Quiet. People walking on verandas across the courtyard flickered through shadows. He heard their footsteps but they said nothing. After he had climbed three flights he came to the door, the right number. He rang the bell there, and heard it ring inside, like a real bell, but nobody answered. He went to a bench and sat down to wait.

He felt hungry. He had been feeling hungry for a while, but it had seemed important to come to the apartment before he ate. He had had no breakfast, and he was used to eating the main meal of the day at noon. When he had waited for several hours, getting up occasionally to look into the courtyard, he walked back down the stairs and began to look among the buildings for somewhere to eat. The only place he found with a restaurant sign was already closed. Too late for the midday meal, too early for the evening meal. He walked around the group of buildings. There were new shops, looking as though they had not yet sold anything. He went back up to the fourth floor veranda.

He had slept badly on the train, sitting up all night, and now he felt tired. He wanted to lie down on the bench and sleep. But that would be taking liberties, he thought. He had not even met the professor yet. He sat on the floor, in his overcoat, and leaned against the bench. Nobody came to tell him to get up, so after a while he lay down. In the summer, at home, he used to lie in the hay in the afternoon and read popular-science magazines until he fell asleep, if he was working alone on a job, as was often the case during the years he had been a roofer's assistant. That was before he had taken over the farm, which was already behind in its taxes and barely fed them, the way things had got. Even as recently as his own childhood, things had been different. Cleaner, brighter, better off. And yet even these days he would go fishing—wet flies in the daytime, and at night poaching in the dark, shallow, fast-running river, setting nets too small to be legal, at the edges of backwaters, in parts of the current he had known all his life. He could sell the catch in the hotels. He worked without a light, because of the police. They all knew him, though they came from other parts of the country. They got to know everything along the river. If they caught him on the bank, or outside his barn, with the nets and fish, they would ask him to open the nets, and when they found the fish below legal size, they would fine him. Depending on who was on duty, and how heavy the catch was, they might fine him more, or less. Sometimes nothing. If there was a new man or they had been told to crack down, they might fine him for possessing a net too fine to be legal. Once they had confiscated a net, but it was an old one, and he had managed to buy it back later, very cheap, through a friend. They never looked into the rusted metal barn, if he could once get the nets in there. Then he could stand in the dark and listen to the dripping, and to the voices in the kitchen, where his mother would be pouring drinks for the inspectors, and watch through the murky window, while the fish flipped their tails in the trickling net behind him. Until the men left, and then he would get out the light and shade it, and start taking the fish out of the net.

He read about fish in the magazines. He thought about their lives. There was an article about their hearing. He read it many times. The author said that fish heard with their whole bodies. Their element conveyed a continuous message to them. They were all shaped like sound waves. All waves were echoes of each other: waves in the sea and in the air; sound waves, brain waves.

He looked at a leaf, one day, and considered its spine, like that of a fish, and he thought of how the whole leaf vibrated in the wind. Each leaf must turn the waves of the air into a kind of sound, though he could not hear it, any more than he could hear what the fish heard, in the water. The author of the article referred to the element in which human beings spent their lives—whatever it might be called.

The young man had wondered why we did not hear our element, whatever it was, with our whole bodies. He felt certain that the shapes of fish were very important in understanding the whole matter. He built a boat shaped like a fish, with ribs laid like fish spines, and he lay in it listening to the current. If you could live that way, he decided, if you could keep those shapes around you all the time, maybe you would begin to be able to recognize the sound of the element in which you were living, passing through you. He made drawings of buildings with spines like fish spines, and curved walls and windows like scales. He used photographs from the magazines of groups of buildings in cities, and he drew pictures of them shaped like fish, schools of fish.

"But I have to be practical," he said to himself. " 'What use would it be?' they will ask. Hospitals and schools for the deaf, first. Start with normal hearing, which everyone agrees about. Try that, first." His designs grew more elaborate. Centers for the Deaf, shaped like fish.

Then he saw an article about a famous architect, living at present in the capital, teaching at the university, a professor who spoke of using in his buildings the shapes found in nature. There were pictures of important buildings that exemplified the architect's theories, and beside them drawings and photographs of natural objects whose shapes he had adapted: shells, grains in pieces of wood, nests. His latest building, as it happened, had been an aquarium, into which he had built the shapes of waves, which he had gathered from different places. The young man had decided to write to the professor about his theory concerning the importance of the fish shape, and his idea for a Center for the Deaf. He had sent a few drawings, to make certain things clear. Why the buildings were arranged as they were, in relation to each other, in a current. "Dear Sir," he began his letter, but the title on the envelope, of course, was "Professor."

He had thought he would fall asleep, but he had lain there in his overcoat, thinking about his plans, wide awake. Maybe the restaurant would be open now, he thought finally, and it came to him for the first time, like the recollection of something funny, that he was farther above the ground than he had ever been. He had known from the article that the professor lived in a tall building like this, which he had designed himself. The young man tried to see what kind of natural form was echoed in the shapes of the balustrades, but he could not recognize anything. The professor had said that mathematics, too, was an expression of nature, and perhaps the tiers of shadowy verandas were mathematically harmonious. The young man made his way back down to the restaurant. Lights were on now, inside. It was later than he had thought. It was hard to tell how a day was passing, in a city. He went in. There was a counter to sit at. No one else was in the restaurant. He imagined the buildings around him shaped like fish, in the gathering dusk. A woman came and gave him a menu, in silence, and he ordered a fish to eat, to see what it would be like here. It was all right. The woman who served him left the radio on in the next room, and stayed in there while he ate, but she came back out as he was finishing, and he paid her, and went out into the lighted spaces curving around the new buildings, and up to the veranda. One small light was burning by the door. He lay down again, beside the bench.

He began to think about his letter—whether he had made it sound clear and correct, what impression it had made. He had heard nothing for several weeks, but he had seen in a paper that the professor had been away for the opening of a building in another country. Then the note came saying, "Why don't you come on the ninth." The young man had imagined many kinds of meetings, and he lay and worried in the dark, thinking, "Why should I worry?"

Then he heard them coming, a group, on the stairs. Young men, young women, laughing and talking. He remembered where he was. A big dog came running up to him, and sniffed him all over, lying there by the bench. Didn't even bark at him. Wagged his tail and went to the door. And the people he had heard on the stairs began to spill onto the veranda, and along to the door, without even noticing the young man, at first. When they did, they looked startled, and stared at him. Not one of them was wearing an overcoat. Shirts, blouses. Some of them carrying jackets. He recognized the professor, from pictures. But taller than he had imagined. The professor did not look as old as he must be, talking fast with all the young people, who must be the students the superintendent had spoken about. The young man stepped forward and told the professor who he was, his name.

The professor looked as though he had forgotten. The young man said his name again.

"Oh yes," the professor said, with no sound of recognition in his voice.

"You said why didn't I come on the ninth."

"You—Oh, are you the—the fish shapes?" The young man nodded.

"Come in. Come in. Too bad you weren't with us earlier. Have you been waiting long?"

The professor had his key ready, and opened the door

without waiting for an answer. The students moved into the apartment as though they were coming home. They turned on the lights, established themselves here and there among the furniture, went on out into other rooms, picked up half-empty wine bottles, found glasses; one opened a guitar case and took out a guitar.

"Let's see what we can find," the professor said, turning to his new guest. "Have you eaten?"

The young man nodded.

"Something to drink," the professor said, and held up his hand as he walked toward the door that probably led to the kitchen. "This is the young man with the fish designs," he said, and left the room. The dog, lying on a sofa, watched him go out, and got up and followed him.

The students all looked at the young man, but nobody spoke. The walls of the apartment were of brick painted white. There was a large fireplace, wide and deep, raised above the floor. One student, who was lighting a fire, had turned to look at him, like the others. A big painting, over the fireplace. The young man tried to make out what it was a picture of. He felt it was much too warm in the room, which had been closed all day. He missed the air of the veranda. He was sure he would not know the answer, when the professor came back with glasses and a question. Where and when would they have a chance to talk, he wondered. He felt certain that he would find nothing to say, and would pass out after a few drinks, but he stood waiting. Some of the students were talking to each other, again. He stood looking at the picture, and at the walls with lights shining onto them, and the large windows in which the lighted windows of other buildings could be seen. He imagined himself as the professor, and at once it seemed to him that he could not hear anyone in the room.

CERTAIN words now in our knowledge we will not use again, and we will never forget them. We need them. Like the back of the picture. Like our marrow, and the color in our veins. We shine the lantern of our sleep on them, to make sure, and there they are, trembling already for the day of witness. They will be buried with us, and rise with the rest.

T HERE was an old woman who lived by herself, up the hill, on Garfield somewhere, or Taylor, near where the paving had not reached, and made shirts that took a long time, so that people laughed about it. They were good shirts, though, it had to be said, and they ought to be. By hand. Like the ones she had made for her husband. There were people who said they remembered him, but if those who said they did asked the others who were present, it would turn out that they themselves were the only ones there who would say they had actually known him, so that it was half way to his not having existed. Surely she must have had pictures of him. If there were any children they were long gone. Sometimes she came if the women's circle was having a sewing meeting, and it was always a surprise, and then it was told about afterwards as though the day had been an occasion. Because nobody knew what she would say next. She got cross and argued. They thought it was funny the way she remembered things that none of them had seen. And she took it for granted that they remembered those things too, which was really what was funny. It was only a farm, up there, when she lived there, at one time. Before they started blasting the mines under the hill, and she heard them. Just grass and trees, then. Animals, and sheds with lamps.

She would walk fast, farther than they ever walked, through the streets that had been fields and pastures and woods, on a snowy night before Christmas, with a shirt held out flat, in tissue paper, for a present, and a cake baked for somebody, and her cakes were famous for being bad. She never let anybody know she was coming. She would not go in. I won't come in. She stood there with the door open. She never stayed to talk. She was so thin that they compared things to her, and she wore an old overcoat and a round hat pulled down to her eyes in a way that people showed each other when she was mentioned. In years to come, some would know, without being told, that she was dead, and some would realize that it must be hard for people to remember her name, even the few that were left who had known her.

She referred the passing weather to the great disasters. She spoke of the blizzard, when it snowed. It never snowed like the blizzard. Did it? Not like the blizzard, though. And she meant eighty-eight. Or eighty-five, whichever it was, they said to each other once again. When nobody was born but one or two. And in the snowstorm she saw the church burn, in the terrible cold. The whole spire catching, and the snow on the ground shrinking back in a widening circle, and them crying. Then the bells fell out onto the stones and smashed like glass, so that she always heard it. That was the year of the flood too. It came after.

When the bells fell, that was the worst, she said, since the burning of the Great Union, and they agreed. They said it themselves. They had heard it said. They knew it. What was the Great Union, and where? Nobody told. They looked away. Some nodded without meaning yes, and some shook their heads without meaning no. Even she had not seen it, whatever she might say. Unwatched by anyone alive, the immense white columns had bathed

60

in flames, and dropped to their knees and faces in fire, reflected on all sides. The thousands of white candles hanging in rings of gold and crystal had melted and flown down through the high burning halls, onto the green marble, and the gilded roofs had hung for a moment in the heat like wings made by humans, and then had sprouted flames along cracks the shapes of lightning, and sagged and tilted, to shatter across beams and rafters, and splash into the piled fire. There was nobody to know whether it all sank in land or water. It must have burned all night, all day. Night and day. There was nobody for it to belong to. The farm had not even been thought of.

Vanity

ONE night we decided to camp in the hills beside a series of waterfalls, and had to speak a little louder than we usually did in the woods. It was later in the day than we would have liked it to be, when we got there. It had rained all day and the grass and bushes were dripping. Just up ahead of us there was a small bridge over the stream. When we had eaten we got ready to sleep in the car. It was going to rain some more.

When it was already night we heard voices. Deep resonant voices of men. The summer nights there are twilit for a long time. We could make out a big old truck parked not far behind us on the same level patch, with its lights out. Some figures were using flashlights to get things out of the covered back of the truck.

If they peered in on us, we said to each other, the tops of bottles glinting in the dim light looked like the ends of gun barrels. They would think we were armed. We laughed. We lay whispering about them, rehearsing what we had heard about local people, and describing the place to each other, the sound, the light, the colors, the past day, in which we had come a long way.

One of the men, who looked very large, in a long raincoat, came over toward us. He looked like a farmer. He wore a sweater and a knitted hat. A big crumpled and swollen face, a protruding chin. He put his face up near the window. After a while he must have seen us. He said "Hello."

So we answered. We said "Hello."

He said we looked as though we weren't from around there.

"No," we said.

Well, he said, he wasn't either. He named a place he had come from, and asked whether we were acquainted with it, but neither of us had heard the name he had said, and so we answered no.

So he started to tell us about it. How far away it was. Its population. What the winters were like. What sort of people lived there. He shone his flashlight into the car and said it looked as though we really lived in there, and he admired that.

He asked us if we were going on in the morning, and we said yes.

"So is we," he said. And he asked us if we had heard of the Bible Meeting at another town whose name he chewed and swallowed, and we answered no. So he started to tell us about that. The road there, what it was like at different times of year. What an event it was for miles about. How they sang hymns he had never heard. He said he was going there to preach. He liked to preach there. He went every year.

He said he hoped we wouldn't mind their staying the night beside us there. He said he had a young man with him who was not right in the head but he wasn't no harm, nor nothing like that. Just so we wouldn't think anything wrong. They would just be getting ready for bed, he said.

He turned away and took a few steps.

Then he came back.

He asked us whether we would be interested to know what text he was intending to preach on. So we said yes.

He raised his hand, and then bent down to the window

to stare in at us.

From the Book of Ecclesiastes, he said. Two, five. He nodded his head. "Do you remember that one?"

So we answered no.

He shook his head, and gestured in the air, and rolled his words, and recited: "*I made myself gardens and parks and planted in them all kinds of fruit trees.*"

"That's it," he said. "*All kinds of fruit trees.*"

"Well, so good-night," he said.

So we said good-night, but he had already turned off the flashlight and was on his way back to the unlit truck and his companion.

So we laughed.

A MAN walked down the street with three dreams for sale. Of course he would not tell anyone what they were. He even said that he couldn't, because the dreams wouldn't be the same for them. He couldn't tell them anything about the dreams at all. They were there like straws to be drawn. Everyone hopes for better dreams than his own, and people bought them. The dreams were to be opened in private, the buyers were told. They were printed on exactly the same paper, which was made to dissolve as it was read, or to dissolve anyway if someone tried to keep it without reading it, like a talisman, so that it might produce its dream that way, as everything can do if the right spirit approaches it. A little later they would return to sight in the man's hand.

People who bought the dreams sometimes met each other later and tried to compare which dreams they had bought. Very suspiciously, at first. Very cautiously, with hints back and forth. Everyone found out after a while that the other person seemed to have bought a different dream. But then it turned out finally that there were too many of them in the same room for them all to have had different dreams, and they started arguing with each other. For they had all seen that there were only three dreams in the man's hand.

But with each person each dream clearly had been different. And still the buyers wanted to know which of the three dreams they had had. They tried everything. They classified by means of every triad they could think of. They divided each other into three factions, which never seemed accurate enough. They kept changing sides, and never forgiving each other. Eventually, in order to check, two of them tried to read the same dream at the same time, and it disappeared at once, entirely, and never reappeared in the man's hand. That happened again and the man was left with only one.

"Now won't the others come back at all?" he was asked.

"No," he said. "But it doesn't matter. They were all copies of the same dream."

"Will you sell us that one?" they asked.

"No," he said. "I'm going to give it back."

"Which one is it?" they asked, almost in unison.

For none of them had learned anything at all. What can you learn from a bought dream?

A MAN was able to get hold of all the laughter in the world, and he packed it tightly and locked it up in his house and hid the key.

The trouble was that nobody missed it.

He had to tell them what they were missing. Nobody knew what he was talking about. Nobody believed him. Nobody thought that what he was talking about was real. Who could believe that, after all? Would anyone believe it if someone came up and said that they had all the laughter in the world locked up somewhere? Would anyone believe it, even if neither of them laughed?

He tried to describe laughter to them. He showed them how it was done. He showed different ways in which different people could laugh. He told them all the things that made people do it, everything he could remember or invent. People falling down. Filth. People making terrible mistakes. People unable to control themselves. Misfortunes of all kinds. People with something the matter with them. No interest.

He told them that it would be good for their health, and that he would not make it expensive for them. No interest.

There were many things about it that he didn't even know, he said. No interest.

It had been called divine, he said. No interest.

But the man kept on trying. Because at least at night he could always go home and take out the key and open up some and have a good laugh to himself. But then one night he started to laugh at himself, and that made him lonely.

He tried to invite somebody else in to laugh. But it was very hard. He even said he would give the laughter away.

At that somebody else laughed.

So that person remembered how to laugh. So that person was on his side. They were laughing together. Somebody else was laughing with him.

But that meant that somebody else had some of the laughter in the world. So he started making plans to steal it.

But the other kept giving it away.

THE things that you lost by the way were guiding you. And you tried to replace them. Which do you think you will see again, them or their replacements? Unless you lost the replacements as well, which some-times happens. And sometimes you had grown to like the replacements better. But sometimes they were hung around your neck in a bag, and taught you and taught you and taught you, like your own soul, and you grew as deaf to the one as to the other. Then sometimes what you thought you had lost turned up again. Even in the bag around your neck. And it was still guiding you, still crying "Repent," from a wild place. But you did not know how to follow it any better than before. You did not attend to the fact that it knew its way in and out of your life better than you did, even knowing where to wait for you, which you would not have known. You did not even consider its having a destiny of its own, woven through yours. Eventually disaster again sep-arated you for an unknown period which neither of you might survive without changing lives at least once. And if you lost it and never found it again, as is most likely, it was something that was never yours to give away, it was a foretaste of total disaster, an absolute nakedness that you could never have conceived of and arrived at without so many guides. But some need only one. Some lead the guides.

So you went on losing and losing, as the rain loses, the mountain loses, the sun loses, as everything under heaven loses. You came alone together and here you are.

T AKING advantage of what he had heard with one
limited pair of ears, in a single and relatively iso-
lated moment of recorded history, in the course of an
infinitesimal fraction of conceivable time (which some
say is the only time), he came to believe firmly that there
was much he could not hear, much that was constantly
being spoken and indeed sung to teach him things he
could never otherwise grasp, which if grasped would
complete the fragmentary nature of his consciousness
until it was whole at last—one tone both pure and entire
floating in the silence of the egg, at the same pitch as the
silence. Next, by measurement and invention he came
firmly to believe that there were high notes which the dog
could hear that remained inaudible to his own ears,
and which the dog had been hearing for longer than he
himself had been hearing anything. Therefore there must
be something in the nature of the dog which the dog had
never understood, for it had not been meant for the dog
alone—something however which he himself would now
understand better if he could ever come to hear it, since
it was for understanding that he had sacrificed hearing.
So he domesticated the dog. But before he learned to
hear the high notes he came firmly to believe that there
were lower notes which the donkey, the bull and the
cow could hear and he himself could not, and he

domesticated the donkey, the bull, and the cow. Still higher notes, and he domesticated the porpoise, the bat, the bee, the ant, and kept all the surviving species of birds in cages. Still lower, and he domesticated the elephant, the cat, the bear, the rat, and kept all the remaining whales in stalls, trying to hear through their ears the note made by the rocking of the axle of the earth. Because by that time, by measurement and invention he had defined a relation in which they stood to each other solely with regard to the frequencies of their limits of hearing, and he had drawn them, according to their frequencies, on a chart, in orderly progression, like a calendar going forward and backward but not in time, even though time was the measure of the frequencies, as it was the measure of every other thing (therefore, some say, the only measure), and across the chart he had drawn lines at the outer limits of what he believed each could hear, tracing a river flowing both ways. And from the chart he could calculate what each of the other existences could hear, though not what it could be: the owl could hear a head turn. Turning his head he tried to imagine what it would sound like to an owl. The bat could hear a hand held out. It took shape in the bat body. All he coud not imagine was the bat. The elephant could hear the roots of a tree, and slept without moving its feet. But the chart did not teach him to hear anything or even how to listen for it. The flattened paper became one more of the promises of knowing for which he had given up fragments of his hearing. Furthermore he had to admit that the animals certainly did not hear the same things, tamed or in cages, that they had heard in their free state. And beyond—and in fact among—the last known animals living and extinct, the lines could be drawn through white spaces that had an increasing progression of their own, into regions of a hearing that was no longer conceivable, indicating creatures wholly sacrificed or never evolved, hearers of the note at which everything explodes into light, and of the continuum that is the standing still of darkness, drums echoing the last shadow without relinquishing the note of the first light, hearkeners to the unborn overflowing. The lines projected off the chart, out into the night. Even from the squares that were occupied by creatures with ears limited like his own, no sound rose. He pressed his fingers against the white panes of the paper, and he thought the vestigial ears in the skin of his fingertips stirred for a moment, but he still could not understand anything they heard. He straightened and turned out the light and listened to the rain.

THE bottom of the lake is standing on its side. It is made of oaken boards planed and varnished. You can tell that there is a slight, steady breeze, for the current of the oaken grain flows slowly up the varnished boards in lines of light. The wood is cracked here and there. A crack is a root, and every board contains memories of roots, and understands, while resisting. The lake hardly delays the light enough to be seen, until one is at a distance. Then its surfaces begin to shine above the already unseen boards, along which the light is flowing in lines, in another world. The eye can never perceive the movement of those lines, and yet it sees that they are in motion. They flow on, to join everything else.

The water is deeper than it looks.

Nearby the waves are echoing against an empty shadowless boat, and the heart listens.

Everything we hear is an echo. Anyone can see that echoes move forward and backward in time, in rings. But not everyone realizes that as a result silence becomes harder and harder for us to grasp—though in itself it is unchanged—because of the echoes pouring through us out of the past, unless we can learn to set them at rest. We are still hearing the bolting of the doors of Hell, Pasiphae in her byre, the cries at Thermopylae, and do not recognize the sounds. How did we sound to the past? And there are sounds that rush away from us: echoes of future words.

So we know that there are words in the future, some of them loud and terrible. And we know that there is silence in the future. But will the words recognize their unchanging homeland?

I am standing on the shore of a lake. I am a child, in the evening, at the time when the animals lose heart for a moment. Everyone has gone, as I wanted them to go, and in the silence I call across the water, "Oh!" And I see the sound appear running away from me over the water in her white veil, growing taller, becoming a cloud with raised arms, in the dusk. Then there is such silence that the trees are bent. And afterwards a shock like wind, that throws me back against the hill, for I had not known who I was calling.

As they grow, out of pure devotion, before long the festivities come to blind us to their occasions, as the middle blinds us to the beginning, when if we could see the beginning we could see the end, where they sit together and nothing is hid between them. We keep remembering something different from what we celebrate, to commemorate a glimpse that we have forgotten, as a stone slab may commemorate a resurrection. There were golden wagons moving without wheels over the desert in a little cloud, with four tall torches lighting the way in the mind of one who saw and tried to tell us. And we listened and made wheels.

T HE bells in the savage mountains make such a tinny
clangor because century after century bells had
to be brought up the mountains, hand over hand, many
sleeps on the way, over huge rocks and steep slopes of
naked stone, climbing stepped gorges, threading cliffs,
crossing deep ravines. And to have bells that were big
enough, they had to be thin. Trains of Indians and mules,
both of both sexes, and both slaves, and eating as slaves,
hauled in the mountains bark cables twisting and groan-
ing, the shoulders of mules and heads of Indians harnessed
to fraying ships' hawsers dragging sleds to each of which
a heavy bell was bound with drying jungle creepers.
They moved upward in the white mists before the sun
came out, the dark gorges aflap with shrieking birds.
And they stopped only when the sun had set, painting
their faces or their backs red as it went. They slept by
the trail, most of the humans attached to the propped
sleds, each by a long chain that led over the bell and
through a ring in the collar of one of the sentries' dogs.
Around them like a second wave of sound, unattached,
slept the ones recruited in each village on the way, as
volunteers, sent by the elders of the villages by way of
tribute, to pay for the safety of the villages. Martyrs.
They all slept under the black trees, around the bells
onto which leaves, acorns, pine cones, unknown forest

objects, fell in the night. The bells echoed waterfalls too far to be heard. The long processions dragged the cavernous heads behind them up into the neck of the rain-forest, down the other, even steeper, slope, across a rugged plateau, and up again into the high basin, to be beaten in the tragic sunsets, blending happily with the old hammering on iron wheelrims of different sizes which had been brought up before there were tracks for wheels or clearance for sleds, and the even older army cauldrons with leather-covered wooden clappers. Some of these survived and still bear the dents that were struck when the first bell was rung in celebration of arrival, before the dogs had finished the bones of those who had died that day in the gang hoisting the bell with ship's tackle into the crossed beams of the patient tower. Even the slaves, in their way, had felt enthusiasm for the end of the achievement, and had stood waiting for the fierce sound hammered out of it in the name of the greatest of silences, henceforth to tell the sun where he was. The bells survived the bearers many times over. When they crack and it does no good to beat them any more they are taken down and stood on the floor, where candles are lighted in front of them, the smoke of myrrh swirls around them like clouds on the mountains, and names are whispered, with different intonations, into their broken places.

A CROSS is a door of the dead. It was always so. Before there was anyone living, it was waiting to bring them into the world. It was the shape it is because of the way each one would be, thrown down or lifted up. Already the cross's shadow was reaching out over the ground, because they come up through the shadow. They always did, to be born, and to be born again. We sit at the threshold. Our shadow becomes part of the shadow reaching out over the ground. There are steps going down inside the shadow, beyond our shadow, but they are not for the eyes of the living, they are not for our feet now. We sit here, and when the dead come up, the first step into the new life is inside us. We sit here whenever we can.

When we die we will walk down into the cross's shadow. Each of us will part three ways. Each of us will come to the end of being seen. We will have gone. Each one's shadow will stay here. No one will see it then. One by one, when we find the turning we will start to look for the others again. It will be dark. It is a larger world than this one, and as empty. But each of us will be looking for the same thing, the same shadow, in the dark of that world, which lies behind the dark of this one. When one of us finds the cross's shadow we will wait for the others, and when they come the

79

three of us will become one, and start to climb. We will come out into a world that we never saw, even though our first step may fall inside the living, who will not see us. Our own shadows will not know us, but we will not need them any more. We will leave them and go on. That will be the life without shadows.

It leads through us.

We feel it. We feel it!

THE mountains are there in every direction. Already we are high up. They are higher, wherever we look. Sometimes the sun goes down behind one, sometimes behind another, depending on us. The mountains rise too steeply to climb, in most places. As far as the mountains, on all sides, there are little courtyards, and tiled roofs, with trees rising out of some of the courtyards. Dogs bark and bark. Balls fly into the air and drop out of sight. Voices of children flutter over the roofs. Roosters who never see each other, answer each other. Immortal storms break around the mountains. There are caves in the rocks. The clouds come down into the gardens at night. For hours at a time the streets are removed. They are folded up and the houses heal together over them. Then if you lay your ear to the heavy walls you may hear a heartbeat.

Meanwhile the streets are put away in the caves in the mountains. They lie there in the dark telling everything they know, without a word, and it is washed away, and they are returned, wet, and ready to go on watching. They are returned, a little washed away, but otherwise the same, and to many the difference is not apparent. In the underground streams everything becomes transparent in the darkness. The only sound is that of running water, and only the streets can hear it.

When the streets are returned, the houses stop breathing, which they can do for long periods of time without its being noticed.

The children who are born when the streets are away remember their own silences. Formerly, in order to rule in the country, a child of the blood royal had to be born at such a time, and so the royal midwife was accompanied by an assistant who remained with an ear to the wall throughout the entire delivery, praying for the streets not to return, not one, not even for a moment. Nowadays this is no longer considered important.

The caves do not listen to the streets, they merely wash away the stories. They know that the streets will not come to them forever to hear the sound of water, and that one day the houses will not heal, and both the streets and the walls will die their next death, which is of the body. Then the water, silent at last, will wear away nothing but faces long since transparent, leaving only the eyes.

At Night

Those who work at night are one body, and sometimes they are aware of their larger self. There are watchmen, helmsmen, surgeons, purveyors, thieves, bakers, mothers, beginners, and all the others. Together they are alive under the presence of the spaces of night, and it seems as though their veins might go on growing out of them into the dark sky, like a tree. They hear a fire differently. There are those who work at night, alone. Only alone. When they work it becomes night, and they become alone, they alone are awake. All places become the same. The worker may be one of the fingers of night, one of the ears of night, one of the veins of night. Even one of the eyes of night, as the eyes are the eyes of day. He or she may be the mind of night, in which all those others are, and their days with them. You forget so much of yourself most of the time, they all say to me so that I can almost hear them. So much of yourself you know nothing about, and never will know anything about, they say. So much of you makes you uncomfortable. Some of yourself you are clearly ashamed of, they say. Well, you know. Anyway, what is wrong with working at night? You have the bell-frogs. You have the owls in the walnut trees. You have the sound of a well. You have the sleepers, with their dreams moving all around you. There are even dreams of you working at night, sometimes. You dream of it yourself. Do you really work in the dreams alone? Do dreams help you to work at night? Do anyone's dreams have any effect? Growing alone into the night all around you.

A Tree

A TREE has been torn out and the blind voices are
bleeding through the earth. Wherever the roots
tentatively learned, the voices flow for the first time,
knowing. They have no color, except as voices have
colors. They do not even have sounds. They are not
looking for one. They come together like fingers. They
flow out. They explode slowly to where the branches
were, and the leaves. And then the silence of the whole
sky is the echo of their outcry.

As I was a child I heard the voices rising. I sat by a
wall. It was afternoon already, facing west, near a tree,
and I had heard them before. All the roots of the earth
reach blindly toward mouths that are waiting to say
them.

Martin

You turn into a white dust road at the foot of a hill, and there is a man up ahead carrying a beam that reaches all the way across the road. He is walking in the same direction you are, but some distance ahead. Five minutes walk ahead. Less. Three minutes walk ahead. Keeping the same distance, never seeing you, though the road winds a little, following the water in the bottom of the valley. There is no one else on the road. There are cows and horses far off in the flat pastures. There are donkeys. There is laundry on thorn bushes grown for it. There is a dome of a church over a hill. There is a cloud of blue smoke rising from behind another hill. There are black birds. There are little white clouds over the mountains. There is water hurrying silently in a stone trough. There is the light of the sound of brass. There is wind. There are feathers blowing.

He never sees you because he never turns. He never turns because he is carrying the beam that stretches all the way across the road. He is carrying it behind him, with his two hands and with a strap slung across his head. The beam is balanced on his back, on the strap from his head, and he goes on walking. He is taking the weight on his head, his neck, the slope of his shoulders, his feet, the backs of his heels, the backs of his legs, his lungs, some little part of it in his hands. He is wearing a coat the color of the road, down to his knees. The long ragged hem keeps whipping in the wind. The long hair on the back of his head is all that ever faces you. But he keeps the same distance.

Though he set out so long ago.

He was born five minutes before you.

If he had not nearly died of sickness when he was three, he would be far ahead of you by now, out of sight, with the beams already in place.

If his leg had not mended, when he broke it in his fifth year, he would be far away now, begging.

If his mother, who was two years dying in pain, had lived another fifteen minutes, he would now be behind you. You would never have seen him. He was not born where you first saw him, and if any detail of his journey, of his whole life, had been different, he would not have been there in time.

If his name had been different, he would not have been there in time.

His name is Martin, but you cannot know that.

If the saint had not lived the man would not have been there.

But this world is not made any other way.

The water is flowing back.

It is not one beam he is carrying, but two.

But he is not tired. He keeps the same distance.

You will not catch up with him to find out what he is doing. Not in a country of beams, rafters, planks, tables, cupboards, benches, chairs, beds, doors, gates, posts, sheds, fences, fires, in which every piece of wood has been stolen.

Brothers

A MAN from Lode had not seen any of his brothers for a number of years, and as the country had suffered invasions and wars and epidemics he was afraid his brothers might have died, or might be in distress, and he went looking for them. After travelling and inquiring for some time, he was commended to a woman who read fortunes, who told him to take the road to the city of Simburad, in the fen country far to the north. The man from Lode had no reason not to follow her instructions, and he set out for Simburad, though he did not know a word of the language of those regions.

Not many people take the road to Simburad, beautiful though the capital is reputed to be. The road is barely a road—a track over sand, or over marsh, crossing fords that can be dangerous even in mid-summer. From the time he passed into the country where the few inhabitants speak the language of Simburad, the man from Lode met no one else who was travelling there, and no one who was coming back. It was a long journey. He was alone, and he never saw any of the people who live in those regions, except at a distance.

He was less than a day's journey (by his own calculations) from Simburad, when he rounded a little hill one morning and saw that the track ahead of him descended once more into marshland, and half-way across a wide fen, among scrub trees and bushes, disappeared. It disappeared. Not only the track—he discovered as he approached it—but the ground on which it stood, for some distance on either side, had been swallowed into the earth. As he drew nearer, he saw that the track led to the sagging edge of a chasm. It was a country of waters, and he was not surprised to hear the sound of a river. He went nearer, to where he could see over the wet, slippery verge, and he saw, far below him, a piece of the road continuing along the floor of the other side of the chasm. It must have sunk in one piece, and remained that way, leading into the far wall of the pit. Nearer to him, on his side of the chasm, a stream was flowing, dark, green, with the heavy, murderous hissing of floodwaters. He saw the figure of a man down by the stream, bending and turning on the shore, as though looking for something—the motion of someone picking over ruins—and from time to time taking what looked like a piece of driftwood to a construction made of sticks, beside the dark stream. The man from Lode could not tell whether the sticks were a shelter, the beginning of a bridge, or the materials for a raft or a fire. The edge of the chasm was boggy and treacherous, and the man from Lode lay down to look more closely. He saw the body of an animal—perhaps a goat—come floating down the stream, and the man below him fish it out with a long stick, and roll it over and examine it, and then look around, upstream, downstream, and up to the edge of the chasm, to where the man from Lode was hidden by small bushes. Something in the face of the man below made the man from Lode happy to realize that the other could not see him. He reproached himself for hiding; he could not explain to himself why he should hide from the man below, but he was afraid to show himself, and he lay still. The man below drew a long knife, and cut a piece off the animal and began to eat it, just as it was, looking up around the edge of the chasm. He turned away at last, and the man from Lode slipped back through the bushes until he could not see the other man's head, and then he sat up and thought about what he should do next.

He could think of no reason why he should be afraid of the man below, but he seemed to be. Certainly he had no wish to stand up and show himself. And even if the other had not been there, how would the man from Lode have got down into the chasm, and crossed the river, and got up the other side? All around the chasm, and on both sides of the road that led to it, lay deep marshland, with mud and water above his depth. He pondered the matter for a long time, and at last decided that he could do nothing except turn back.

He returned the way he had come, and he met no one for several days. Then one afternoon a man came toward him on the road, travelling toward Simburad. The man greeted him in another foreign tongue—not even the language of the country of Simburad. This other was well dressed, and vigorous, and affable. They smiled and bowed to each other, and after a few fruitless attempts at conversation, laughed, and went on in opposite directions.

But then the man from Lode thought, "He thinks I've been to Simburad and am coming back from there." And he thought he should warn the other about the chasm, and perhaps spare him several days journey, for that road, after all, could no longer be said to lead to Simburad. So he turned and went after the other, and overtook him, and tried to explain about the chasm, and the river, and the man gathering sticks and carving up dead animals to eat, though even as he described it he could not explain to himself why he had hidden.

But the other traveller could not understand anything that the man from Lode was trying to say. He stood listening with an expression of polite indulgence that gradually turned to one of embarrassment, then one of boredom. The man from Lode redoubled his efforts to make him understand, speaking more and more simply, slowly, distinctly, repeating a few phrases over and over, with gestures whose emptiness he could feel as he made them larger and larger on the echoless air. He could see the other's patience give place to a suspicion that the man from Lode was the victim of some more or less acute mental disturbance, a suspicion that became a conviction when the man from Lode seized him by the arm to draw him back, away from the direction of Simburad. The other pulled himself free with a threat, and hurried on his way. The man from Lode ran after him for several minutes, repeating the same useless phrases and gestures toward the other's retreating back, and then he gave up for the second time on the road to Simburad, and turned back.

And the other travelled on over the sinking road, and came, after several days solitary journey, to the hill, and the marsh, and the chasm, and he crept to the edge and lay down and watched the swollen stream and the man below gathering sticks and bodies of animals, and the man's face frightened him, and he drew back to think of what he should do next, and decided to give up the journey to Simburad, and as he stood up and started back he remembered the man whom he had met, whom he had taken for a fool, and it occurred to him that all this may have been what the man from Lode had been trying to tell him. He wondered whether he would ever see the man from Lode again, and whether he would recognize the man if he found him, and whether they would be able to tell each other anything.

The Fugitive

THE land of the fugitive is all around us. To someone each of these trees is a thing to hide behind. Each of these rooms is a place of concealment, judged essentially in terms of how well hidden someone would be in it, how long it would be good for hiding in, and how someone could get out of it. Each of these streets the fugitive watches with a view to passing along it unperceived. He would rather swim in a river than in a lake, and in the river and the lakes you can see why. He moves from body to body, and most of them admit him like a shadow, and a hollow is conceived inside their heels. The greatness of the flight does not depend upon the fugitive but upon the pursuer.

The fugitive never forgets the smell of dogs. And what is music to the fugitive? Above all things he hates his brother, the pilgrim, who walks on the ridges and rests under the trees, dissolves the rooms and the streets, and worships the rivers. The greatness of the pilgrimage does not depend upon the pilgrim. That is the family likeness.

To the fugitive a cave is a place of defense. A desert is only a danger. There are fugitives with children. The children are surprised at nothing. There are fugitives who collect animals, and tame them, and try to teach them to do everything that men can do. To a fugitive even a disease may be a place of refuge, since he was already hiding in his body. There is a picture of him as an infant, learning to walk, with his arms up as though he were trying to fly.

The sleep of the fugitive is all around us.

But it happens that he wakes into his brother.

The Good-Bye Shirts

DAILY the indispensable is taught to elude us, while we are furnished according to our wishes with armories of what we do not need. And like all armories, they wait. None of us needs a good-bye shirt. But which of us (if a man) is without one? The lack of one, to our eyes, would be a matter for pity ("Poor thing, not even a good-bye shirt") or for contempt ("Not even a good-bye shirt") or for the perfunctory expression of horror elicited by murders and grotesque accidents ("Not even a good-bye shirt") or for the prophylactic amusement used for saints ("Not even a good-bye shirt"). So in each of our cupboards there it lies, no doubt, or will lie, and we do not even know—we may never know— which one it is, any more than we knew which would be the meeting shirt, though we may have tried and tried to choose it. And what guides our hand at last? If we could be said to know what we were choosing, would we ever put on the good-bye shirt at all? Or would we put it on at once? Have we in fact already worn it repeatedly, through the casual farewells of days that have faded out, one behind the other? Are we wearing it now?

When two good-bye shirts meet each other, at the laundry, or on the bodies of their wearers, what lack of recognition (as far as we can tell) even at the moment and in the very gestures of routine parting! But then, are we ourselves prompt to recognize those who share our calling, our fate? And the shirts, the real good-bye shirts, can be certain of sharing only two things: they have owners; and they can be emptier when worn than when waiting in the cupboard or hanging on the line in the sunlight, waving.

WHEN I went to sleep among the late very poor, as a virtue, I took with me only what I considered indispensable. Everything else I had sold, as we have been commanded to do, and the proceeds had been given to the poor. The old poor, the poor of all ages and of every kind I could recognize. I made a study of the poor—from the standpoint of financial superiority—and by this time I had with me a single suitcase, and a book I was reading, about birds. I saw that all the cubicles opened directly off the hall and each was painted a shade different in color, the shades in orderly procession. But the spectrum of colors was not complete. The other end was not red, but just where the red should have begun was the wall of the shower room: pink. The light was on in the shower room. I saw, where doors were open, as we passed, that the cubicles had no windows at all, which I thought was important. I saw that they were painted the same color inside that they were painted outside. Of course they were small—hardly wider than the door—and I thought that was important too. I saw the soles of shoes, socks, and feet. I was given the room at the left, on the end, next to the shower. It too was pink. I had already paid. They had probably already locked the outside door. Old men were in the shower, taking showers. They were telling long stories of their childhoods that they had remembered only as they were coming down the hall, and the more they told the more they remembered, continuously without listening to each other, with the showers on. I did not want to shut the door, and I did not want to go into the shower room in the middle of the old men's shower. I sat in the pink cubicle, on the edge of the cot, and waited for them to finish. It was the longest shower I had ever heard. Each of them kept remembering other long stories out of his childhood and taking his time getting the facts right. I could hear about one word in five, which sometimes kept recurring and recurring. Only one of them sounded as though he had his teeth. They would get to laughing and start coughing, and then all take up coughing for some time, and then have a pause, and remind themselves of something and start off again with after-coughing voices, and sighs, through the sound of a tropical down-pour, while the roaches ran into the beam of wet light under the door.

I had had the foresight to relieve myself before I went in, and for the time being there was no urgent reason for me to leave the cubicle. The only light in there was a tiny bulb embedded in a heavy wire cage, that would not turn on at all with the door open. When it was lit it was so faint that the book had to be held up almost to the wire, for the print to be made out at all. Furthermore, the light was at the level of my knee, at the edge of the cot, on the end wall: I had to hold the book down and peer over the bottom of the page. The light made a small ivory circle that did not reach from one margin to the other, and the book had to be moved back and forth. I came to a picture of a night-blue bird, but the light would not show the whole bird at once, and I had to move the book in all directions, around and around, trying to remember the rest of the bird as I went, and never managing to visualize it all, while the noise of the old men in the shower came through the closed door just as though it were still open.

If I shut my eyes the voices grew louder. Then there was the noise of people running down the hall and flinging open the shower door with a crash, greeting, some of the stories starting off again, and suddenly loud argument for a while, and then the sound of someone being sick, and the others shouting instructions and comments in the rain. I went out into the hall and could see the bodies moving slowly in the foggy glass. The light was out in the window of the office, near the other end, and the door at the far end of the hall was open. I walked quietly back along the colors, each of them like a shadow of the one before it, while the light from the shower room threw my own shadow the whole length of the hall, and my head and shoulders disappeared in the dusk at the far end. As I walked I saw empty cubicles, nothing in them but the cot. And I looked in—nothing. The noise from the shower room grew fainter and the air seemed better—cooler at least—as I got farther away. All the cubicles with open doors, with no one in them, were empty of belongings: there was just the cot. No one seemed to be in the dark green office, but there was another of the faint lights in the wire armor, burning above a table inside the window. The last cubicle of all, deep blue-violet, was vacant. I went in and sat down and it was like having a room near the sea at night. The noise from the shower room was like the breaking of an occasional wave. I lay down and shut my eyes and then thought I must ask if I might have this other, new, cubicle. I wondered whether it was being saved for somebody: the first one inside the door, on the left as you came in, opposite the lockers. I had not put anything in my locker, yet. It occurred to me that the deep blue-violet cubicle might be used by somebody connected with the management: so near the office and the outer door. Someone who had odd hours. I looked to see whether anything had been pinned to the walls, signs of prolonged occupancy, but it was too dark to tell. With the cubicle door open, and the door at the end of the hall open, I even seemed to get a little breeze there, stirring up the stale air, and that seemed important. I thought I had better go and ask at the office before I fell asleep in the dark blue-violet room, and I got up and as I went out thought of leaving the book to claim the place, and then laughed at myself and realized how tired I must be and how late it probably was by then, and I went out and stood in front of the office and peered into the dark green room with only that bulb like a reflection on an ornament, and what little dim light from the shower room came that far. After a while I could see that the desk was locked with a bar and a heavy padlock. There was a massive lock on the inside door. I wondered how I should go about waking up whoever was on night duty, and then I realized that there might be no such thing. I could see that it might not be easy to rouse anyone from the other side of the locked inner door. No light shone around it. The voices were still going on in the shower, with no change. I thought of giving up and going back to the pink cubicle, and then I thought that would be silly. When there were other empty cubicles where I stood a chance of sleeping, getting a night's sleep like everybody else. I stood listening to the old men's voices pulsing steadily down the hall. Finally, when I had almost forgotten what I was doing, I tapped lightly on the window. Nothing happened, and taking courage I was about to tap again when from an inside window that I had not been able to see, beside the inner door, a flashlight was shone onto me, and I thought I saw a thin man in a bathrobe. I tried to explain with gestures what I wanted to know, and for a while the flashlight shone on me steadily. Then another very small light was switched on inside, and I saw the man: long unshaven, a tattered dark maroon bathrobe, pale blue rumpled pyjamas. And he held up a long finger and made a negative gesture, probably meaning that the desk was closed, and that he would not speak with anyone at that hour. Too late, too late. In that case no one else should be coming for rooms; it might be alright for me to take the blue-violet cubicle, unless it was occupied by someone to do with the administration, and I thought I had better just make certain about that, so after a moment's bracing myself I tapped on the window again. Nothing happened. I raised my finger to tap again, feeling a welcome impatience, when the flashlight beam leapt out at me again. But as soon as it had picked me out, before I could make a single gesture, it went out, and I was left with my mouth open, about to pronounce the words silently for him to lip-read. But when the light went out I just uttered out loud—I did not shout—the word "blue." The light did not come back on again, though I went on gesturing for a while. And when I looked down the hall I saw that several of the doors had heads sprouting out of them, watching me.

"What did you want?" one of them asked. I could not see which one it was. The voices in the shower were going on just as before. The heads in the hall were outlined against the light of the frosted glass door of the shower room. I ignored the question as well as I could. Then someone else asked it, and then another. It sounded as though they were all asking me, and more heads came out, and doors opened.

"Nothing," I said.

"It's down there," one of them said, pointing toward the shower, and some of them laughed.

"Do you know whether anyone uses the room by the door?" I asked calmly, addressing myself to the nearest head, in its own shadow.

"Which room?" somebody asked.

"The last one. The dark blue-violet room."

"Blue what room?" somebody else asked.

"That room." I pointed.

A voice said "Purple" and then other voices repeated it with faint echoing satisfaction.

"Is anybody using it?" I asked again.

"Why do you want to know?" one of them asked.

"I'd like to change my room," I said.

"Why?" they asked.

"It's quieter up here."

"Have to ask," one of them said, and others agreed.

"They won't talk to me," I said.

"Too late," several of them said. The flashlight shone on me again, and then went out. I turned and gestured again. When I looked back down the hall, most of the heads had gone back into their rooms, and others disappeared as I stood watching. I decided that I might as well simply take the purple-blue room. If someone to do with the administration came in later and found me in his bed, he could always wake me then. By that time the old men in the shower might have gone to sleep, even if I had to go back to the pink cubicle—or I might find yet another empty room somewhere in the greens and yellows. Of course my key would be to the locker that went with the pink cubicle, but that would make no difference. I went back down the hall quietly, with no one paying any further attention, and into the pink cubicle. My suitcase was gone. Nothing else had changed —the sound of the pelting shower, the voices. I sat on the cot. I looked under it: nothing. I went and looked out in the hall. No one. In a moment of helpless rage I stepped to the shower door and pulled it open. There must have been eight or ten of them in there, but only two or three were in the shower stalls, in the steaming showers, their bodies hidden by slabs of echoing white marble, only their gray heads and occasionally a thin soapy arm appearing over the top. The rest were sitting along the wall and against the showers, wrapped in towels, in the steam. They were shouting back and forth. It was the one place where the light was any good and they could congregate. They all stopped their stories to look at me, in my clothes.

"My suitcase has been stolen," I said.

"Suitcase," one of them said.

"Just now," I said. I heard the word repeated behind me, and turned to see that the heads had sprouted again.

"My suitcase, yes," I said to them all.

"Should put it in your locker," one of them said.

"Didn't you get a locker key?" another asked.

"What did you have in it?" another one asked, and I wondered whether he didn't know. It seemed to me that nothing could have happened without them knowing it. But then I told myself that all anyone had to do was to walk into the open cubicle and pick up the suitcase and walk out with it as though coming back from the bathroom. I let the frosted glass door shut, and heard the voices begin to laugh, and then the stories begin again. I shut the door of the cubicle behind me. I still had the book in my hands. I turned on the light and tried to make out a sentence or two. I gave up and turned the light off and opened the door a little and lay looking up in the shady pink light. There was supposed to be ventilation. I thought I could hear it, over the noise of the shower. Then I must have gone to sleep, because I was wakened by someone opening the door of the cubicle—which must have closed—and gray daylight coming in. The man who opened the door was one of the people who ran the place, but I had not seen him before. I supposed that he was on the morning watch. The shower was off, dripping. The daylight came through the frosted glass. I got up and went out, and along the hall to the office.

The window was open and another old man, in a collarless shirt, was at the desk.

"Good morning," I said.

He returned the greeting without looking up from his paper.

"My suitcase was taken last night," I said.

"Suitcase?" he said, still not looking up.

"Yes, I had a suitcase. Everything I had was in it."

"Should have put it in the locker," he said.

"Perhaps somebody took it by mistake," I said.

"What do you want to do, press charges?" he asked, looking up. No expression at all, pale eyes. I looked down the hall. One or two men in towels, going back and forth to the shower room.

"It's only that there were things in it that I needed," I said.

"What?" he asked.

I did not answer right away. "A toothbrush," I said. He reached into a drawer and got me a new one.

"They're given to us," he said. "Complimentary."

"Thank you," I said. "But there was my razor too."

He got out a complete little shaving kit with a razor and blades and soap and brush.

"Thank you," I said. Then after a moment: "But there was my sweater too." It was cold outside.

"We've got some things here," he said, and reached over to a box of clothes by the inside door, and dragged out a big sweater fresh from the dry-cleaners and threw it at me. I stopped asking. I went back and sat on the pink cot for a while, thinking about the other things that had been in the suitcase: underwear, socks, shirts, papers. I discovered that my virtue had ceased to be important to me, and I got up and went out to continue my study of the poor from a different point of view, no longer knowing what was important, and aware that there were aspects of poverty that I had never dreamed of. All that I had was a book about birds, the clothes I was wearing, not all of which I had chosen, a new toothbrush, a shaving kit that I had decided not to use, and whatever was in my mind.

Who has been to the top of Hunger Mountain and seen what can be seen from there, and returned? The view of The Promised Land. Most who have come to tell went only part way. Many have died part way. And even they have seen things that no one else ever saw, things they could not describe, too hard for the words, and then too hard for them, the witnesses. But certain ones who never forgot and who never sleep gave us their words to eat. They buried their words in us and went away, leaving us hungry, part way.

The Entry

WHEN he has been walking for so many years why is his sack so heavy? And in those woods which he thought he knew so well. But he is older, and lost. The paths have gone. He does not know where he is at all. At last he comes out on a rise above a railroad track. Down there between the banks the snow is still drifted. It is spring, but the snow is still deep there. More spring snow may fall tonight. A train comes by, south-bound. Passengers look at him. Some point him out. He looks at himself. The train has gone. He walks on, along the tracks, northward, until he sees a station ahead of him. The ties, from which the snow, here, has melted, look like a flight of stairs going neither up nor down. He does not even know what he has in his sack.

THERE was a boy in a country now much changed who had a very curious and shrewd nature but could not imagine his own faults.

There had never been a road between the place where he lived and the capital. Little was known of the capital, and that little was rumor—no one where he lived had ever been to the city. But they had all heard of a girl there who was more beautiful than anyone they had ever seen.

It was decided, where the boy lived, to build a road to the capital, and men labored like ants, cutting through the forest, making ditches and bridges, passing places that they had lost, making mistakes, leaving blind alleys cut into the mountains, bridges half finished or collapsed, turning back, setting off again—because none of them knew the way to the capital. It was a long and tortuous road, and it was finished at last, but that is not the story.

The boy had decided that he would marry the beautiful girl whom they had all heard of, in the capital. When the road was finished, even before it was opened, he was the first to set out on it. He travelled day and night, and survived all the mistakes, and found his way back from the blind turnings, and one night when he was utterly exhausted but was almost in sight of the capital, the moon rose, and as it did someone ran past him going the same way, and was soon far ahead of him.

As soon as he thought about it, he knew that the other must also be going to the capital to court the beautiful girl, and would arrive long before him, and tell about him, tell everything about him, and win the girl before he himself even appeared, ragged and late. He began to imagine what the other would tell. For the first time in his life he began to envisage his faults one by one, starting with those that were not real, and then going on from there, little by little, because he could not stop. He walked along in the moonlight, at first crying, and then laughing.

The Crossroads

I HAVE come to the crossroads twice now. In the end there is no way to name, as though to fix forever, the way the light can differ totally between one time and the next, in the same place. The difference is eternal. I can only imagine the future of light as something like the light I have known, when in truth it will be totally different, of course. If, as it may be, there is to be a third time.

The first time there was the green little boy. I came alone and when I stopped at the crossroads he emerged from the dark woods on my right. The sky was dark to show that he was not real yet. An effigy made of moonlight. But he knew me, and was expecting me. He would guide me in the dark, but he had no features. He needed my eyes. He would have to be a sleeve and I would have to be a hand going to wear him, groping. The hand of a child.

The second time there was the red little boy. It was daytime to show that he was not real yet, emerging in the same place, out of the green foliage. An effigy made of red cloth, the same shape as the first. He would take me to where I was going, but he had no features. He could not even stand up. He needed my life, to go into him like a body into an image, and go with my threadbare hands in front of me. The life of a child.

Each time the crossroads, as I later realized, was a day of my existence that I could not account for. And I did not even know what part of the day I had forgotten, that had let all the rest drain out—its number, its name in the week, its season, its saint. But each time I entered it and passed through, by what apparently was the only way. As a child. Even so, if I reach the crossroads another time, I do not think that there will be three of me, but only one, again, in totally different light. And of an unknown color.

A Cabin

The cabin is set into the huge treeless slope, facing west, toward the yellow evenings. From below it appears to be almost at the top. From above it appears to be less than half way. The sunlight enters through the open door and falls on the rough table and earth floor. It rests a hand on the ashes of the fire against the dug-out eastern wall. In the spring, late in the day, light is reflected from the slope outside onto the blackened beams. Then the cobwebs light up the corners. And then for weeks the sound of the stream at the foot of the slope reaches to the door. The wind rides over it, tramples it, but it keeps on, climbing, with the words brought from the ice, the clear consonants. In autumn there are whole days of stillness, in which voices from unseen throats drift in the air, calling sheep. The only neighbors live far out of sight on other slopes. When they pass they stop at the door. Their faces are red from the wind. Their hair has been mown. Everything about them is broad. They stand on the sill and laugh, describing the unlikely mind of authority, telling of involved triumphs of their own which never happened, raising their voices because of the wind. They leave, pronouncing invitations that are pure formalities.

FINALLY the day arrives when I watch myself coming back after years abroad.

By that time I am living in a little blue house of my own, up on a hill overlooking the harbor. There is a pergola of grapevines outside the back door that faces east, up the hill. Nothing a stranger would call beautiful: the pergola is a structure of plain iron struts set into the stucco house wall and threaded with heavy wire, from which in late summer the grapes hang. At the outer ends the struts rest on the posts of angle-iron that hold the heavy galvanized chicken wire of the garden fence. More grapevines in the garden, and beyond them tomatoes, peppers, eggplants, endive, leeks recently watered, beans both for drying and for eating green. The area outside the door itself, in the perpetual shade of the vines, is cemented over: a place for a long table and benches, painted gray. A few books and pencils on the table, the less precious books left out even at night, much of the year, in that climate. On the far side of the cemented area, a cemented wall a yard high, separating it from the garden; the wire fence rises from the top of the wall. On the wall, along the fence, there are pots full of flowers—some of which have been there for years, and have been cut back and re-potted in black earth, in the same pots. Bushes of basil in old

III

square tin cans. Broken knives, spoons, forks, a wine glass without a stem, a pair of broken scissors lying on a rust mark shaped like scissors—a shadow in an eclipse —tucked among the pots. A ball of string, reposing in a little ring of spattered dust. Nasturtiums clambering on the wire. Sun dazzling on the vine leaves. The garden gate a framework of bent galvanized water pipe covered with the same heavy chicken wire as the fence; rusted hinges that screech when the gate opens, a rusted latch that clangs when it closes, and both sounds are parts of the gate, as anyone who knows the gate can tell. A white rag, thrown over the top of the gate, is rotting there. The yellowish gray wall at the foot of the fence is covered with the grain patterns of the planks that framed the space when the cement was poured. A long fading map of one section of a bewildering mountain region. The boards themselves have long since fed some fire. Empty bird cages on the wall, left by a former occupant, and kept, obviously, for no reason, as though there might be some other use for them. Resident spiders and lizards in the wall. I spend more time out there, as it happens, than I do on the other side of the house, on the roofed terrace facing west above the harbor. Every room of the long narrow cool house looks out to sea.

In the mornings the sun is welcome, slanting under the vines of the pergola, outside the kitchen door. And in the afternoons, when the day is hot, it is pleasant to sit out there with the sun beating on the other side of the roof, and the vine leaves sifting the glare, until the shadow in the garden suggests that it is time to begin work there.

Inside, everything is equally simple. Few possessions have survived the years, and those few are either useful or have their age and origin to commend them. A patchwork quilt that I remember from childhood. What would it mean to me if it were seen again only now, after the lapse of many years—half a life? Would it mean anything to me at all? Would it even be familiar? What enzyme of experience might have dissolved it in my mind? The books are more recent. And I no longer have the devotion to them, the individual objects—as though they might be pieces of a raft that I had in my early youth. But it is hard to imagine myself not knowing each one of them, never having seen any of this. I will never be able to explain it.

A steep path leads up to the house above the vineyards. There are no houses above this one. Beyond the garden is the dry hill: thorny bushes, and then the open pasture rolling away to the mountains of dark oak trees and gray limestone. What would it look like to someone who perhaps had grown to dislike walking? Horses wander up the path in the evening and chew at the wiry bushes, which continue to spring and thrash from time to time in the first hours of darkness. I try to imagine what a city must be like now. It is no use. What kept me?

And the others who have come and gone in this house since I came here to live. Women, a series of friends, whole lives, and my lives with them. To know nothing of all that, all those years on the other side of the planet, where it was night when it was day here. What can be told of such things, to one who never knew the people but only the names? What do pictures mean to those who never saw what they represent? What judgment can the ignorant contribute? What will anyone know of all this in the future? What will they be judging except themselves? How do I know, for what can I know of them, and what pictures they may have kept? I am try-ing to imagine myself, on the basis of ancient, unsorted recollections, approaching the coast, on the last day of the voyage, after many years. What was it that I never thought I wanted, that kept me away there for half a life, promising to come back but not coming, perhaps believing myself happy? Was I?

It is a long voyage, and all morning the ship can be seen from the terrace on the hill, making its way across the metal sea and into the channel behind the break-water. Half a day, all afternoon, for the men with cables and winches on the sea-wall to ease it up the nar-row twisting channel, conceived for nothing larger than fishing boats, turning it around the eddies and pockets made by the tides, into the wide still harbor. It is almost evening, the hour of the first coolness in the shadows and the first premonitions of the long blue-and-yellow twilights, before I start down to the harbor, leaving the door unlocked, but then turning in the path outside, after I have closed the gate, to put my hand on it again. Well, I have done that before.

Then I go down the lane slowly, to the place where it becomes cobbled, past the weavers' houses with lengths of woven woolen cloth, brown and ivory, hanging out on wires—which nearer the houses also bear grape vines —and chickens scratching under them. And the houses of old women whose vineyards are tilled by neighboring families in exchange for most of the wine, so that the old women look at the vineyards in the daytime as though they already belonged to someone else, but at the ends of the day they look at them still as the vineyards of their infancy, peopled with all the figures of that time, over which the old women now stand much taller, and much lighter, beginning to rise and fly away. Past the houses of those families of half shepherds and half fishermen, some of them taking turns, where I go more and more often to listen to the stories. After all my own travels, from which I always came back. I go on down to the cobbled steps, the marble cobbles, worn smooth, scratched by the horseshoes. Down past houses with hens on the balconies under hanging laundry, and door-ways into leafy courtyards, where water is running.

I arrive at the open space along the harbor as the last cables are warping the vessel to its berth, in time to watch the late sunlight on the crowd waiting to see the ship dock, though they know no one aboard. It may fall to me to be the only one getting off here, I don't know. I feel cool, and as though with all my youth, standing in the shadow of an old tree by the harbor, watching the ship in. But it may not be so with me after the days of confinement on the ship, with its dull woodwork, its alien paint, its carton cabins. No one has been able to get in touch with me for a long time. The voyage has been good for me, the days of silence. What was it that held me so long, and will it call me back again to the shrieking of metals held in the hands, and the days like stammering? It was part of me. It sent me here, which is not to say that it will leave me here. It never left me anywhere before. Eventually the horizons were aching to part again. There was the expectation of some absolute encounter. The thought of women. Who has it all been calling? What will it be like here? What will I be like? Knowing nothing of so much of my life, and the lives of others that have been woven into it. How can I ever know anything about them from words and a few photographs? What do I remember, at this moment, about myself?

Everyone knows who is coming. There will be no delay at customs, and the trunk, which is said to contain little besides a few clothes, books, notebooks and photographs, will be taken to the one hotel, with its columned lobby full of palms, and its glass reception desk. Neither of us was ever a frequenter of cafés, but there in the café of the hotel we will sit, with a bottle of wine, in the evening light, looking at the harbor, trying to come to know each other as we are now, after all. To know each other well enough to judge, as tentatively as possible, whether it would be better for me to come up the hill at once, and have the trunk (which I remember, laughing) brought up in the morning, or whether it might be as well for me just to stay at the hotel for a while, and we would then have dinner, and after dinner I would go back up there alone.

The Roof

THEY turned, on the roof, and noticed each other, and each wondered whether the other had come up here first, and had been up here all along, but not seen, not noticed, around behind the black cabin, perhaps, where the stairs emerged from their well through a door that was tarred on the outside. Or whether the other had come up later, stepped through the doorway without being heard, approached on the fine gravel fixed in tar, and stood there looking, for very long. Two men, both of them young, though not in their first youth. Both thin, and unhasty. Then the taller, darker one, in the old jacket, found that he was seeing the other, who was blond and in a red sweater, as a little boy, sullen and hoarding himself. The face still preferred to look down. And the one in the red sweater noticed that the other one had been observing the new tomb. Then the taller one, in the jacket, smiled, and greeted him.

The one in the red sweater asked him if he was looking for something. Up here.

The other one answered that he was the sculptor.

The first one said oh that was all right. He said he was the gardener. And that he was surprised they had not met.

Each moved slowly and hesitantly to shake the other's hand, and looked away. The afternoon was over. People were on their way home from work. Some were home already, sitting down in the first chairs. The gardener gave a laugh and said you could hardly call it a garden. Small cypress trees in sooty tubs. Long boxes containing cropped evergreen bushes. He explained that the Fire Department would allow no more, and added that he was amazed they allowed any of it. He asked whether the other had come to look at the sculpture, though he already knew the answer.

The other nodded, as though smoking a pipe.

The one in the red sweater would hardly have called it a sculpture, either, until that moment. But, as he said, he didn't know anything about those things, and they didn't interest him. Just the same, he wouldn't have called that a sculpture. Standing on the new tomb.

The sculptor said he had come up to see it at this time of day. They both stood looking west, over the city. A saffron light was filling the sky, and a few clouds were passing over, like silent trains.

The gardener asked him what they thought of his sculpture, and the sculptor said nothing for a moment, and then asked him who he meant. The gardener simply pointed down beneath his feet, so that the sculptor could only have guessed whether he meant the inhabitants of the apartment building, the officials of the cemetery, the immediate family of the person whose body was in the new tomb, or the general public. Not the older dead, at any rate, behind plaques in the parapets of the roof. The sculptor shrugged and said he guessed they thought it was all right. They were going to have an unveiling, he said. Or they'd talked about it, anyway. But it had been so long since they said that, and they'd all seen it by now, he wondered whether there was any point in having an unveiling. He'd thought of taking a picture. He didn't have a picture of it. The gardener asked him whether he had come up to take a picture, and the sculptor said no.

The gardener asked the sculptor how they had heard about him, and the sculptor said he wasn't sure. They said they'd seen something he'd done.

The gardener asked whether they had told him what kind of thing they wanted on the tomb, what they had in mind, and the sculptor said no.

"They just let you do what you wanted," the gardener said, and nodded, to himself, to show that he was familiar with such liberty.

The tomb stood out from the wall like a marble bed. The first stains had appeared on the white stone. At the far end of the tomb, against the parapet, was a head-stone of slate with edges uncut, irregular. Blank, no name on it. Behind it, the city: higher buildings, bridges, pigeons in the smoky sky. On the marble pedestal formed by the tomb was a life-sized baby carriage. At first it did not appear to be fastened to the marble. One of the gardener's objections to it, to begin with, was that he thought it looked real.

He said he had been surprised when he had heard that they were actually going to bury somebody up there. Nowadays. He said he sometimes came up just to have a look, too. At the view. Three years, he said, he had been working there.

The sculptor asked him if he'd done all that, pointing to the tubs, and the gardener said he had. There had been nothing there. It took three of us to move some of those, he said. Up all those stairs. You have to be careful where you put them. Over the joists downstairs. On top of structural walls. Otherwise the roof wouldn't take it, he said. He was afraid the Fire Department wouldn't allow it, but they never said anything. Of course, it always *was* a cemetery, he said. But not for a long time. And it was one thing in the old days, but he'd never thought they would actually bury somebody else up there, now. He asked the sculptor if they just came and asked him, like that.

"They called up and came around," the sculptor said.

The gardener asked him whether they had told him anything about the individual he was to make the sculpture for, and the sculptor said they hadn't.

The gardener asked him when they paid him, and the sculptor said it was all right; they did.

The gardener asked him whether he had designed the whole thing, or just the monument part, and the sculptor said just the monument and the headstone. The tomb was already there when he came up, the first time.

Was he going to put the name on the stone in time for the unveiling, if there was one?

"No," the sculptor said.

Wasn't he going to put it on? At all?

"No."

The gardener turned away.

What did the family have to say about that?

The sculptor said he hadn't asked them. "They know who it was," he said. And if anybody else wanted to know, they could start inquiring, and that way it would mean something to them. He asked the gardener if he remembered names from cemeteries, and the gardener said nothing.

The gardener had objected to the fact that the baby carriage was painted, all bright colors. They spoiled the effect of the whole roof, he thought, every time he came up to tend the plants, and sweep. He asked whether the sculptor had a key, or what, and the sculptor said he did.

"They just come up here on week-ends," the sculptor said. And the gardener said yes, and maybe birthdays and like that.

"Or else the Board of Health," the gardener said. He had thought they might have to take the whole thing down again, tomb and all. He had never thought they would allow a funeral up there in the first place. Those others, in the old days, that was when the laws were different and people didn't know so much about things like that. As it was now, they must have had to have all kinds of special vaults or something to satisfy the ordinances. Or a lot of pull. But how long would that last? He guessed they wanted to keep them in their own building, he said.

But he kept thinking the Board of Health could change their minds even yet, and make them move it out of there, and then the Fire Department might make them get rid of everything else.

"Maybe," the sculptor said, and asked him where he worked, and the gardener named the richest addresses.

He had wondered whether it was, in fact, a real baby carriage, and since he was alone with it the first time he saw it, he had gone over to inspect it, and had touched the push-bar, and the springs had not moved, the carriage had not rocked. He had decided that it was bound to fill up with water in the first rain, but then he had looked inside and seen that the blankets and pillow were all molded and painted, and that there was a drain in the corner, that ran down under the carriage.

"I even heard somebody wanted to tear down the whole building," the gardener said. "Put up something else. Higher."

"They're always going to do that," the sculptor said.

The gardener said he wondered if they thought of burying any more up here.

The light was going out of the sky. The colors on the carriage were darkening. The sculptor turned his back on the tomb and said it was nice up here. He said the gardener must have really made a difference.

The gardener said it had just been a garbage dump.

"I've been up here in the morning," the sculptor said. "First thing."

"I always knew this place up here," the gardener said. "They called me up, one day, and said somebody told them about me, and they needed a gardener. A gardener, though. As soon as they told me, I knew what they meant. But I like it. I come when I want. I believe it's the family themselves," he said. "The owners. Decided to fix it up and use it themselves."

"I guess so," the sculptor said. "They said it was their building. When they were around to see me. I just came up here once to look at where they wanted it put, with a couple of them. They were relatives."

"I think they have some kind of pull," the gardener said again.

The sculptor nodded. "Did you see that thing about it in the paper?" he asked, and laughed. The gardener said he hadn't seen it.

"I did it in the studio," the sculptor said. "And I want to see it in place, different times."

He looked around again, at the roof, the tomb, the lights coming on, the sky growing dark, and started toward the door to the stairs. The gardener picked up his tool bag and followed him. They stepped over the high metal-covered doorsill, onto the tiles, and the gardener turned on the light inside.

"You always want to lock it behind you," he said, as he locked the door, before they started down the stairs.

The Watches

One of the people I have come to know since I have been here is a priest in the small town. We speak with difficulty, in his language, very slowly. We sit at his kitchen table over herb teas that he brews, and stale tea biscuits, or over bread and fresh cheese, depending on the day of the week. His mother lives with him in the bare presbytery. They say little to each other; speech scarcely seems to be necessary between them. He has read a great deal, carefully, and kept his good humor. He tells me stories of the region, a detail at a time, with much questioning on both sides until I understand each part. Laughter, and moments of blank fatigue. Comprehension of a stage of the chronicle is a thicket opening slowly in the woods. Told in this way the stories begin to take on the momentous intangibility of legends; episodes echoed from an unknown sacred text; parables. Sometimes it is hard for me to understand what he thought was funny. Sometimes he appears to be a little foolish.

I mentioned the acquaintance in a letter to a close blood relative of mine, who I knew was interested in the church. I suppose I did so partly to boast of such an association, particularly as I knew that she had always considered me irreligious. She spoke of it, perhaps out of similar motives, to a priest of the same faith as my friend, who was known to her circle. He got my address from her. He was about to take his vacation. He came to visit me.

He was blond; bald but still young; tall and sonorous and assured. He spoke the language much better than I did. He was affable. He was wearing a neat well-cut gray suit which scarcely indicated that he was a priest. He went to the hotel to change into a cassock, for our visit to my friend, at the church.

We found him in the sacristy, at that hour, at a table under a shelf loaded with empty jars and volumes of old registers, receiving visits from his parishioners, like a country doctor. And in fact, in the recital of their misfortunes they asked for his opinions on medical matters, rather than send for a doctor. They left the three of us alone, and I introduced the stranger.

My friend the local priest welcomed him eagerly, broke out an ancient half-empty bottle of homemade peach cordial, and when we had touched our glasses to each other and sipped, brought from the depths of his cassock an old silver watch, on a silver chain, and held it up. I had never seen it before. It was embossed with flowers all over the back. A white enamel dial, with Roman numerals, like columns. The silver flowers and leaves on the case were worn down, as on the face of an old coin. He handed the watch across the table, to the visiting priest, with a speech about presenting it to the other world.

The visitor accepted it gracefully, admiring its age. Then he bowed slightly and took from his pocket a silver watch, the twin of the other—as I saw when he held it up—and with an identical chain, both of them new. And he handed it across the table with a smile, and they shook hands.

After that we sat down on the benches, facing each other across the table, and there was a brief, stiff conversation, comparing church conditions. The visitor said that he would not be staying in the town. He was on his way south. He became somewhat hearty. We got up to go. As we left I thought him affected. When he had changed back into the gray suit again he seemed more so: the way he held his head, with the large nose and puffy eyes; the way he talked about his travel plans, and all the places where he had been.

The Invalid

THROUGH spring evenings when others find reasons
to walk out under the trees, and through summer
afternoons when almost everyone dreams of lying by
a river, and through each season and each hour in turn,
the invalid sits preparing his case. He is dying. Everyone
knows it. But he has been dying, and apparently at the
same pace, for some time now. For a number of years,
in fact, as we realize occasionally, always with an aston-
ishment which indicates, as much as anything else, that
we have come to take his situation for granted, and it
has become a habit of our own. Yes, he is dying, but
neither he, nor the doctors, nor anyone seems to entertain
a precise notion of how much faster than the rest of us he
is dying, and whether his present prospect of life is to
be thought of in terms of months, years, or decades. Some
prefer to express the matter another way, and say that
his life has been shortened, quite definitely it has been
shortened—but this is scarcely a more helpful way of
putting it. It appears to imply that he, and everyone,
has, or may have, two distinct fates, a possible one and
an actual one, and that the former is somehow measur-
able, a function of averages, perhaps, of norms, and that
the actual thread of existence can be held up and meas-
ured against the so-called possible one, in advance, and
found to be shorter, and for a known reason. This way

of putting the matter, like the other one, makes it clear that what the invalid has lost may be no more than a particular, but unmeasurable, expectancy, or some right to it that had never been altogether beyond dispute—a nebulous treasure, as the successive rounds of the invalid's case have emphasized again and again.

Still, it is generally agreed that he is dying faster than if it had never happened to him—the little mistake which he claims was no necessary part of his life. And apart from the mental anguish caused, as he maintains, by the loss of his expectations, what is left of his life has otherwise been severely curtailed. He is full of discomforts— some of them severe, sleepless, worsening—that might not otherwise have been his. He is the victim of a catalogue of incapacities which he insists were not his before. And those pursuits of the flesh which are still open to him are now empty, in a way he had not before noticed, of ease, and contentment, and joy. But the defense maintains that he cannot prove that he ever possessed most of what he declares he has lost, but that these things are illusions, of which, in many instances, he cannot even claim to be the author.

The event on which the argument turns is not even dignified—a plea which the invalid has not, so far, had the wit to put forward. He was born in another country and brought here by his parents (since deceased) in the first years of his adolescence. It was a painful change for him, one which he does not seem ever to have accepted wholly. Three decades later he still speaks with an accent. He was always shy, frail, ill-co-ordinated, and a hypochondriac. He is intelligent, received a good education, held a series of well-paid and responsible positions, never married, lived alone, talked (whenever he spoke of himself, which was seldom) of the country in which he had been born as though his homesickness had never healed at all; but though his financial and business circumstances would have made it easy for him to return there, he never went, but put it off, put it off. And so for years, until his life seemed as set as the sizes of his clothes; and everyone who knew him was startled when it became known, several years ago, that he had gone back, for the first time, on a visit to the old country.

Perhaps he would have been reticent about the visit itself whatever had happened. As things turned out, it was quite effectively eclipsed by what it led to. As he was returning to this country after a month or so, the customs officials became suspicious of the assortment of medicines in his baggage. In the first place, there was a surprising variety, for an apparently healthy individual. And then the quantities. He had taken from this country a large supply of certain medicines he was in the habit of using, so that he need have no fear of running out even if he were to stay considerably longer than he had originally planned to. Some of these he was bringing back, of course. Several large bottles had not even been opened. Then, while he had been in the country of his childhood he had rediscovered remedies which had been administered to him, or had held his attention, in his early years, and he had tried a number of these, and laid in stores of a few of them. Furthermore, he had tried a series of remedies from the land of his origin, for the ailments that were uppermost in his mind, and had been pleased, in some instances, with the results, and happy to think of taking back with him a provision of those restoratives. Finally, he had consulted several doctors in that country, had thought highly of a number of their prescriptions, and had taken the precaution of procuring quantities of these, against future complaints. When the customs officials began to question him on the subject of this collection, they were not reassured (to judge from the sequel) by his behavior. A hypochondriac can scarcely be expected to plead hypochondria, and he was no doubt evasive, contradictory, nervous, perhaps even irritable, in his replies. They detained him while the bottles were taken away for laboratory examinations. He was not put under arrest and was not allowed to call a lawyer, and his state of nerves while he waited probably did little to allay their suspicions. When at last he was released it was without apology, rather curtly, with a few impertinent remarks about his collection. He had grown accustomed to better manners, in the country of his birth.

It was not surprising that by the time he reached the place where he was living he felt that several of his chronic and recurrent complaints had been inflamed by the incident, coming as it did on top of the fatigue and strain of the journey. He was convinced that he felt crises of more than one of these complaints approaching, and one of the first things he did, before opening windows or mail, was to give himself full doses out of the appropriate bottles, with a little for good measure in each case, because of the circumstances, and then another little bit extra to spite the government officials, with their grossness, and their rude remarks inferring that his medicines were not only unnecessary but afforded him some eccentric pleasure.

The symptoms which began to appear almost at once were not those of any of the habitual ailments, nor of the side-effects to which he was accustomed in the use of some of the medicines. They were new, and alarming. A hot pain blared suddenly in the pit of his stomach, echoed very shortly by another in his head; and this latter was followed by a darkening of his sight, which increased until he could not see out of one eye at all, while the other was filled with flashes and a dim blur. He suffered from nausea, and an extreme weakness of the legs. Between bouts of vomiting he managed, despite his impaired vision, to call a doctor, who was some time in coming. By the time the doctor arrived the symptoms (a racing pulse, and chills, had joined the first manifestations that all was not well) were still more pronounced, and there were moments when the patient swayed on the brink of consciousness, and felt himself drifting out over the abyss. The doctor wasted a few more minutes trying to fit these signs of trouble to what he knew of the patient's medical history, and his subject was rapidly growing fainter before he stumbled onto the right track and began to examine the bottles carefully. The customs men, whether in the laboratory or outside it, had evidently put several of the medicines back into the wrong bottles, and the patient, as a result, had taken the wrong doses of at least two of them—doses dangerously large, and of specifics that should never have been taken together.

For some days the patient's life was in doubt. The sight of one eye was never fully restored, nor the patient's former strength and vigor. The invalid continued to be subject to frequent attacks of vertigo and palpitations, to a complex of shifting pains in the abdomen, head and legs, and his digestion scarcely merited the name. He was unable to go to the office, and though it was possible for him to perform some functions of his old job at home, he had to be content with this, and with a reduced salary. And he, and those who knew him, were led to understand that he could never recover from this new condition, and must expect to die of it.

Of course he brought suit for damages, high damages, and though the first round was contested with considerable callousness (possibly with a view to recording arguments that might forestall appeals later) he was awarded part of what he sued for. It was more money than he would ever have been likely to earn, but he was not satisfied. He brought suit again, for still more money, declaring that his health and his former expectations of life were beyond price, and it was then that the case turned brutal, and the defense maintained not only that it was impossible to establish that the medicines had been put back in the wrong bottles by the customs officials, but also that nothing which the invalid claimed to have lost had ever really been his. And now he spends all his money on lawyers, and in devoting what time remains to him to proving that he was deprived of health, and the prospects of longevity, and the infinite possibilities of existence, by the agency of other people; that these things were once really his; and that he had known them and enjoyed them and realized that they were worth a great deal, even at the time.

Path

WATER laid out the streets of the gray capital, and day after day the rain falls into place along the pavements, and follows a design that is known to it, natural to it, and older than the first buildings, preserved now as bones in reliquaries, inside stone monuments built over them against the weather of the latter days. North of the mountains and the inland ocean with its long seasons of low skies, the city began, doubtless, as a margin of driftwood huts gradually outlining the shape of a hand or hands, where a river meandering through wide marshes chose many ways to the sea. Ricks of branches. In time, rafts. Eventually the shore-haunters brought stone down the river, for building in the color of the winter sky, and the flecked hewn granite began to wander at the water's edge like hems of the light.

The original settlements along the water line, huddled in the dark winters, must have been the stick-nests of clusters of hunters who pursued the retreating glaciers northward, killing along the new-born pastures. Deep in the ice a goddess of spring kept moving toward them. They called her with drums. They listened for her heart and heard soft hoofbeats in their sleep. The surviving legends all tell of journeys, leading out of earlier journeys, between hidden skies. The oldest lyric fragment that has come down to us, in the principal archaic language of those regions, likens the dome of heaven to an upturned boat in which we will embark once again, at the end of time. But that is a relatively late production. It is clear from the legends that the first arrivals came on foot: the travellers in all the ancient stories walk. There are reflected glimpses, in those narratives, of other roofs, by former shores: suns remote forever, older rivers, perhaps even the Nile Delta with its seven mouths, seven fingers, seven candle flames.

The stone facades still float in the rain. In the course of my visit it fell incessantly, beating on its temporarily buried places, and the days shortened, one by one, with a measured suddenness. I was beginning to think I had learned all I could learn, for the time being, of the nomadic legends of that region, and their recurrence in the later levels of the language. I knew more of the dominant archaic tongue than of the current local one, but I knew neither of them well: it was a rare phrase, from any period, that seemed transparent to me, and I was more conversant with the words' transformation than with their sounds. But the directors at the national library behaved toward me as though my interest, in itself, were a contribution to their archives: they put their entire collection, and all the means of consulting it, at my disposal, and the most celebrated philologist and literary historian in the capital, who spoke my language as his own, guided me through the centuries of what I thought of as evidence. As sometimes happens when one is helped lucidly but without interference, his response to my interest, the material he produced, the order in which he provided me with it, and his own commentaries, gave me a sense of our having worked together before. It was plain from the start that he understood what I was looking for—grasped it, perhaps, more clearly than I did, since he held in his mind, in detail, the whole extant body of texts, whereas I had only an intimation of what I believed must be there. And despite the difference in our ages (at least a generation, and probably more) years and exact learning had neither raised an insuperable barrier between us, nor rendered him brittle: he could not only guess what would amuse us both, in the morning papers as well as in the ironic turns of the recorded past, but from our first session onward he was able to put in my way, one after the other, resemblances, associations, traces, clues, the components of recognitions, which fed and warmed my enthusiasm.

We had almost finished going through his compilation of the old documents which he considered most relevant to my interest. We had proceeded in an order that was roughly chronological, and had come to the last of the materials he had set out, several weeks earlier, for me to study. I felt the weight of the approaching winter, and was looking forward to leaving and taking with me the mass of notes, to try to find out what they meant to me, when I had got them back to where I was living. One morning, as a gesture of anticipation, I went to the center of the city, to get my travel ticket, just to have it, even though I meant to leave the date open for a few more days. I walked, though it was raining even harder than usual. The traffic splashed and roared along the winding avenues, metal-boxed processions hurtling through smoke, hesitant chain-saws in water. I tried to keep to the back streets where there were almost no vehicles, though I risked getting lost, since none of the streets ran parallel, but branched off from each other —systems of veins. The closer I drew to the center of the city, the emptier the back streets became. Some blocks were closed to all motor traffic, with vertical lengths of iron pipe rising at intervals from the asphalt. In one such curving passage two waiters under a bare awning frame were carrying stone table-tops indoors. Down the middle of the narrow street an old woman was moving like a dark mollusc: her back was the same shape and color as her umbrella, and her legs appeared to have shrunk into the rest of her. She was carrying a patent-leather shopping bag. The rain ran off her and dripped at her feet. She was walking so slowly that I imagined, at first, that there was something the matter with her. I thought I was remembering her but could not recall having seen her move. It made me feel that I was walking too fast. The rain travelled down her coat and shopping bag rapidly, pausing but indifferent, as on a pane of glass: the gait of a mumbled rite. I was anxious to get to the travel agency, and then on to the library, but I felt reluctant to splash past her as though she were not there. For an instant it seemed that I should do something for her, yet I knew the next moment that the impulse was vain and absurd: she was certainly not helpless; there was no plea in her bent carriage, no despondency in the shuffle of her boots, nothing in the set of her that would have recognized pity. I slowed down, as I passed, and turned to nod to her. The waiters had gone in; we were alone on the street as on a country road. I looked, for a moment, under the umbrella and the dark hat-brim, into a face weathered with age, brown as wood, gaunt and merry. Bright blue eyes. She looked at me, smiling, perhaps laughing. I had assumed that she was doing her shopping; the sight of her face made it seem more likely that she was simply taking her usual walk, inspecting part of her estate, as she had been doing for longer than anyone there could remember. I was about to greet her, but hesitated and said nothing: I had been looking at her out of my own language, and suddenly was overtaken not only by the awkwardness and embarrassment with which I spoke the language of that city, but also (as I realized only after I had gone past, and left the street) by an uncertainty as to what phase of the language,

from what age, was properly hers and would be cor-
rect, if I were to address her. As I nodded, I heard the
rain, above the sounds of the city.

I was late getting to the library. For the past week
and more my mentor and I had been meeting in what
was called the refectory. The materials that he had as-
sembled for me to study had overflowed his own mari-
gold-yellow office in the interior of the rambling edifice.
We had moved to a table by itself at the end of a
reading-room, but we could not talk freely there. One
day we were invited to the director-in-chief's office, a
spacious eighteenth-century room with huge windows
of square leaded panes evenly filled with the gray light
above the harbor: that side of the building faced onto
a margin of shrubbery and a quay where a large warship
was moored. The director sat with the light behind
him. I had met him at the beginning of my visit: he had
been amiable, helpful, and lofty. His manner to me,
when I entered his office, was deferential and friendly,
as though in the interval we had seen a great deal of each
other. Another man was sitting beside him, near the
desk facing us, in the light, wearing a gray-blue gab-
ardine overcoat and a hat. He was introduced to me
as one of their best-known authors, a man whom the
director had particularly wanted me to meet, he said,
because of my interest in their literature, on the one
hand, and because, on the other, his visitor had recently
acquired a reputation as a song-writer. The man was
cordial, featureless, his voice toneless, his questions and
remarks—I thought—unlit. Neither of the reasons given
for our introduction seemed to account for it. I wondered
whether we must resign ourselves—whether I must resign
myself—to being interrupted by a series of such well-
meant (perhaps) but pointless diplomatic encounters;
my friend the philologist thought not. He explained to
me, in his glancing but incisive fashion, as we returned

along the corridor, that I had been repaying a favor. My friend had told the director-in-chief that we needed more room, and had suggested the refectory, which was not in use. The director had hastened to comply—he was more or less bound to do so with any request coming from my friend. But the invitation to his office had been (simple sociability apart) a re-establishment of the director's position of authority, after the favor he had granted. It had served to remind me—and consequently my learned friend—of my obligation. It had allowed the director—who also occupied a high post, and entertained further ambitions in the Ministry of Culture—to put on a small show of his own importance for the popular author, while seeming to flatter him. My friend did not think that the performance would be required twice, and (in exchange) we would have the refectory to work in for the remainder of my visit, and we would have it to ourselves.

He was waiting for me there, when I arrived, by taxi, with my dateless air ticket. I hurried through the reading-room, in my wet coat, and through the small Gothic door at the end of it, and shut that behind me, in the huge somber hall, with a long deep breath and a moment's sense of homecoming, such as I had not felt in the place—or had not noticed—before. The high windows, here, were made of much smaller panes than those in the director's office. They were narrower and longer, the frames rising into stone trefoils and sharply pointed arches. Just above them were the massive transverse beams, the lowest level of the elaborate nest of rafters disappearing into the darkness of the ceiling. Neither the function of the hall nor its history were clearly defined. Part of the building, apparently, had once been a monastery, which had been almost wholly demolished. Sections of the library, much later, had been built in imitation of the earlier structure—or rather, in imitation of drawings, themselves ancient, of its ruins. A row of venerable, faded, ragged flags, on long poles, projected over the room from the stone pilasters between the windows. They were older than the hall, and retained a stillness of their own. The polished surfaces of the two enormous parallel tables flowed out of the shadows at the far end of the hall, to fill with the cold light of the northern morning, and appear to be made of it. At the near end of the table on my left, fixed and bathed in that same light, were the piles of papers and folders that my friend and I had been using —I was startled to realize how much of my own unfinished work I had left, day and night, in that relatively public place. Yet not so public, either, I reminded myself, thinking of the locked door, the key in my pocket, and my friend sitting there waiting, reflecting the glassy table and the spread-out papers. He appeared not to have noticed that I was late, and I did not have a chance to ask him how long he had been waiting: he brushed aside my apologies, smiling about something else. He said that there was something he had been preparing for me, and for which our work until then might be considered a background. He referred, in a rapid summary, to the particular circumstances of historic scholarship in the last century—at the end of which he had been born. I had considered, and in fact remarked at one point upon the irony of our studying the early texts and the older reverberations reaching us through them, in the echoing hall that had been built, in emulation of the Gothic age (a time far more recent than the oldest of our texts) at the very period when the surviving motifs from the Gothic era and earlier were vanishing, just as interest and inquiry were first revealing how swiftly and completely they were receding. He referred me to some of the most ancient neo-nomadic fragments and travellers' songs, and read a few passages

aloud to me several times so that I would catch the
cadence of the archaic meter—the foot, the cadence
itself, he insisted, even though, as I knew, the meaning
of a number of the words, in those fragments, was now
lost, probably forever, and the actual pronunciation
was, to an uncertain degree, conjecture. He left me
studying the texts that he had just read aloud, and a
commentary on certain of their allusions, and told me
that he would be back later. I was used to working alone
in the high empty hall, where the shuffling papers, the
pencil on the table, and my breath, echoed and re-
echoed, and I paid no attention to how long he was
gone. The clock in the tower was striking as he opened
the door again, but I had not noticed when it began
to strike, and so could not count the strokes. There were
two small boys with him, whom I could not at first
tell apart, except that the one was slightly more blond
than the other.

They came in without speaking, and the boys stood
looking up into the rafters, even after my friend had
told them to come to the table and take off their coats.
They did neither. One after the other he led them over
to me, the blonder of the two first, and introduced us,
in their language, of course, and they held out their
small hard hands. I could read no expression in either
of their faces. They remained between me and the
windows. My friend told them to sit down wherever
they pleased, on one of the benches, near the piles of
papers. The one whose hair was darker sat down in
front of me, with the table and the open books and
notebooks between us; his eyes ran over them, and over
me, my hands, my pencil, my face, with the same de-
tached alertness. The other boy sat down at a bench
beside the far table, nearer the windows. He was turned
toward us, but still looking up at the shadows in the
ceiling, and the files of flags retreating into the darkness.

They were twins, my friend explained to me rapidly, in my own language, and he instructed me to sit still and say nothing. He began to talk to the boy opposite me, courteously, respectfully—as he addressed everyone, and as he would have spoken to someone of his own age. He told the boy that he had been thinking a great deal about the poems that the boy had told him (the word "tell," in that language, means both "recount" and "chant") at their last meeting, and that he was as interested in them as ever, and would be grateful if I could hear some of them. The boy said nothing, but looked at me.

My friend asked him whether he remembered those poems, and the boy said that of course he did.

And others? Yes, the boy said, there were many.

Would he tell us one about the dark traveller?

He was in all of them, the boy said.

Tentatively, as though pronouncing the first phrase of a foreign language to a native, my friend quoted a few words, an opening. Something to do with the echoes of a foot on ice. The boy sighed, looked up past us at the wall opposite the windows, and began to hum and pat the table with the palm of his hand. Then he started to recite. His voice was pitched like a string on which the words were played at intervals. He hummed be-tween them, and chanted them as they came, shaping them to fit a pattern that was recognizable but never quite predictable. The poem was a ballad of some kind, or so I thought, though it did not seem to keep to the metrical form of any ballad I knew in that tongue—or in my own. Missing many of the words, as I did, there were whole passages that I could not catch, but felt as though I were following at a distance; then a piece of narrative would emerge, and disappear again—someone walking in a mist—and I could not be sure whether the sense kept escaping me because of my inadequate knowledge of the language, or because of

the boy's pronunciation, or because the poem itself was
difficult. As it was: full of sudden turns, knotted phrases,
kennings, allusions to episodes and characters unknown
to me. The story, or the parts of it that I could catch,
told of the dark traveller's encounters with a series of
lights and a gleaming otter, on the marshes; of his ar-
rival at a frozen fortress, with a fountain of ice; of meet-
ings with helpers (the otter may have been one of these)
and a fight with the first of the ice-giant's dogs. The
traveller relied on the help of spirits some of whose
names he did not know, some of whom he had en-
countered on earlier occasions, in human shape. He
transformed himself, for protection, once into a cloud,
once into something whose name I did not understand,
in which he was frozen for some time—and there again
I lost the thread. The idiom of the poem was con-
temporary—as nearly as I could tell. I could detect
neither archaisms nor literary usages—in fact, it seemed
to me that the language was not, in the usual sense,
even literate: I could make out certain ungrammatical,
"incorrect" locutions of the current street languages,
and bits of recent slang. Once or twice I thought I heard
echoes of a popular song a few years old, but I was not
certain of that. I would have been interested in the per-
formance however crude it had been, but in fact it was
presented with pure authority, and from the start two
things about it impressed me above all. First, the poetic
power of the words, even when I did not understand
them. And then, through the poem's sound and urgency,
the distant but unmistakable beat of those same ancient
fragments which my friend had been reading aloud to
me earlier in the day.

Excited and alien, doubting even what I thought I
understood, I must have been told it in a number of
different ways before 1 grasped the fact that the dark
traveller, the central figure in the apparently endless

poem, was the second toe of the left foot, who had been called The Black Toe ever since he had been frozen. But whose left foot? The other twin listened, without a sound or a change of expression.

The recitation came to an end—or a pause. My friend thanked the boy and asked him whether that was the end of the poem. The boy said no, it was just where he wanted to stop for a while.

I saw that my friend had been taking rapid notes, in a phonetic shorthand partly of his own invention: I recalled, as though noticing a coincidence, that it enabled him to write the sounds of the language at each known phase of its development, and I found myself glancing across at the symbols, trying to see whether I could read them. He saw me looking, pushed some of the pages toward me, and brought a small tape recorder out of a shoulder bag. He began to explain its purpose and operation to the boy, who looked at its operation without obvious interest. My friend demonstrated the use of the machine, talking into it, playing back his own voice, distant and hollow in the echoing hall, and both boys laughed. He recorded their laughter and played it back, the last seconds of it: a tail vanishing through a doorway. He asked the twin who had been reciting whether he would tell a poem into the recorder, and the boy said nothing, stared at him, picked up one of the pencils and began to copy one of the shorthand symbols over and over on the margin of the page of notes. The other twin looked across, from the far table, and watched; though they were not facing each other, both of them laughed at the same moment.

My friend told them that it would take him a minute or two to prepare the tape recorder. He said it as an invitation, as though the operation of the machine might be something that they would like to watch—and they did, but they kept their distance. They began to talk to each other, not whole sentences, but phrases, allusions, half of them in whispers, making each other laugh. I understood little of what they said, and in my own language asked my friend what they were talking about. He told me that most of it escaped him too, as the boys meant it to. It was a semi-secret language, which apparently they made up, in part, as they went along. But he said that in any case they were alluding to things which they alone knew: family circumstances, street games, school. The machine did not seem to be running satisfactorily, or my friend had not mastered its controls. It clicked and whirred and burst into passages of frantic gabbling—glimpses of treble multitudes in panic-stricken flight, old haste of dry water—and while he stopped it and started it he spoke to me rapidly in my language, as though discussing the recorder, explaining to me that the twins came from a mountainous region farther north—he avoided saying the name of the place, so that they would not know we were talking about them, but I noticed them listening to the strange words, while they continued to make a game out of their own.

Their mother had been a young woman from that region who had come to the city as a child, with her parents, during the war, and had returned to the country some years later, with a man about whom not much was known except that he had been a legendary figure in the resistance. He had died, there in the mountains, before the twins were born, and their mother had brought them up by herself. No one had yet determined their exact age, but they were thought to be about nine. Their mother, too, had died, some years before our meeting, and the twins had been housed for a time at a farm of some relatives of hers, in that same region, but at a distance from their earlier home; later they had been brought to their maternal grandparents, in the city. There they had lived for a year, without being sent to

school: fed and clothed adequately; allowed to run in
the streets—until their existence came to the notice of
the authorities, who looked into their situation and set
about resolving what they described as the problem of
the boys' education. The twins had a rudimentary ability
to read and write, picked up at home, from their mother,
and from observation of their elders: they were quick
and alert and remembered what they chose to. But they
were several crucial years older than the other children
whose formal education was no more advanced than
theirs. The authorities waxed anxious over the boys'
associates: they wanted to make sure that the twins
would be able to find friends of their own age. They
feared that the differences of background, of sophistica-
tion, would isolate the boys and further retard their
assimilation. They need not have troubled themselves.
The twins were soon running what amounted to a gang
of their own—posing new problems for the anxious
educators. Their schooling required a special arrange-
ment: the twins sat through an hour or two, every day,
of the ordinary classes, never called on for answers,
though much of the teaching, whether or not they were
aware of the fact, was directed at them, as at a pair of
silent judges. And a tutor was found for them, ostensibly
to help them catch up with the studies of the children
of their own age—or what their age was assumed to be.
He was a man acquainted with the region where they
had grown up—a student of it, indeed, who had been
spending his summers there for over a decade—and he
understood the dialect, which the twins still spoke with
their grandparents. He got along well with the boys,
was more interested in them than in their schooling, and
it was he—among those responsible for the boys' educa-
tion—who had first heard the poems. He had thought
them remarkable, and had brought them to the attention
of some of his learned and literary acquaintances, who
had shared his enthusiasm; it was in this way that my

friend the philologist had first heard them. He told me that the boy had at one time made poems in the regional dialect as well, but apparently had not done so for some time, and no one was certain whether he remembered them.

"But are they really his own?" I asked.

My friend gave me an oddly blank look.

"Does he make them up himself?"

"We don't know that," he said. "We don't know at all."

"And the meter, the ballad form, the rhythm, those echoes of the ancient poetry?"

My friend shrugged. He said that none of those things had been encountered by the folklorists in that region—or anywhere else. He wanted to record whatever he could of those poems, he said, before the twins were fully literate. There would be time to analyse them later.

He seemed to have the recorder working to his satisfaction, and he asked the twin who was sitting at our table whether we could hear some more poetry, with the machine listening. The twins had been laughing and whispering together; now the one who had recited sat back again, looked up into the darkness, took a long breath, and began to hum. My friend switched on the recorder. The boy started to pat the table, sometimes with the palm of his hand, sometimes with his fingertips. Then the words came, the chanted beats, in a voice deeper than the boy used in talk. It was the same landscape as before—a low sky, an ice fountain. Far away on the horizon, a fire, under the night: the house of a planet burning. The Black Toe still unfrozen, in this poem; not yet named, calling toward the fire. A water-flame coming to help him, out of the sky. The boy stopped.

The philologist stopped the recorder, re-wound it, and started to play back what he had just taped. We heard a crackle of static—perhaps scratches on the tape.

Then echoes from the room. Then the humming, but deepened and overwhelmed with reverberations: a series of hollow beats like steady thunder—the boy's hand on the table. The poem began, beyond the rumbling and the echoes, as though coming through water. The words —to me, at least—were incomprehensible. But the boys were laughing, both of them. They laughed as loud as the noise of the machine, slapping their legs like old men. My friend turned it off. He tried to explain to the boy that the machine was not working as it should. He asked the boy whether we could hear that part again, when he had it running properly, and had moved it off the table.

"No," the boy said.

My friend asked him whether it was just that he didn't want to say that poem again, and the boy, in a caricature of the scholar's gesture a moment before, shrugged, and the twins laughed.

Would he say another poem for the listening machine?

"No," the boy said.

Didn't he like the machine?

The boy shrugged again, looking at his brother, who shrugged too.

My friend began to explain the purpose and mechanism of the machine in greater detail, and how it should work, if it were running properly. He asked the boy what he objected to, about the machine. The boy said he didn't want to be turned into *that*.

"Into what?"

"That noise," the boy said, pointing to the machine. "What came out of there."

"But you laughed," my friend said.

The boy shook his head.

"Don't you want the poem to be there?" my friend asked.

"No," the boy said.

"Why not?"

"I won't go in there," the boy said.

My friend put the recorder away.

"What if you forget the poems?" my friend asked.

The boy looked at him without expression for a moment, and then smiled—an impudent, ironic, mocking smile—and took a deep breath again, looked up, began to drum on the table. It was a different beat, more intricate, with syncopations, rhythmic pauses, and after a minute or two I became aware that the other twin was patting the other table, in those pauses. Between them, on the two long polished surfaces, they were beating out a single rhythm. Then the other twin began to hum. I glanced at my friend the philologist, who looked as surprised as I was. I saw the other twin's lips begin to move, and the voice came, lighter but more urgent than his brother's, and with the same power of feeling, the same unquestionable echoes of the ancient rhapsodic diction. His landscape was brighter, but the story was as fierce, full of teeth and blades. The second twin's chant paused, and the first took up the recitation in the name of The Black Toe, running on ice; the boy's words trailed off into lengthening, distorted syllables, and a long wail of loneliness like three descending wolf chords. Then his brother continued, and I understood that his hero was the second toe of the right foot, The White Toe, so called because he raised his face out of the dust, out of the shadow. In one of the episodes he was disguised as a cripple, and his brother rescued him; it was implied that the rescue also happened the other way round. There were calls of warning, triumph, incitement, between the two voices. When the second twin also had ended his words and his humming, and both of their hands were still, the two tables went on echoing, vibrating—strips of gray daylight running into the darkness at the end of the hall.

ONE day an old man was digging in his garden when he turned up a rusty iron box. It seemed frail with age and he tried to open it and as the lock gave a little he pried harder and harder and suddenly found that the lid had come away in his hand and that there was nothing under it, and that his other hand had disappeared. Then he heard the box shut and he was at the end of his garden, and the sun had not yet gone down, and the spade was hanging up, and both of his hands were on the gate.

M ANY of the family tombs are neglected. Iron doors stand ajar, rusted into their quadrant tracks, rust flaking from lower panels molded with reliefs of wreaths resting on crossed arrows. Hinges solid as sculpture. Snow of rust on the echoing floors. Nothing to steal. Broken vases. Dry flower stalks, held with green wires. Portable cement wreaths with the word *Regrets* running around them. A quiet which is neither of the city nor of open country. The few sounds, such as the barking of an old spoiled dog, seem to be coming from farther away than their visible sources.

Small groups of people, all of them past middle age, cluster on benches, talking. It is the day of rest. It is clear that many of them meet here every week, weather permitting, after visiting the family tomb. On some benches those at the ends, of either sex, sit forward and talk across those in the middle, which makes them all look as though they were laying plans, in the shade. It also makes them broader. They wear warmer clothes than the day requires. On other benches everyone sits back and faces out across the walk and among the tombs, even when someone is talking, which is not always the case.

One woman, plump and merry, comes with a small bright-colored bucket containing scraps from her dinner, which she feeds to the cats that appear at the sight of her, like gods. Then she takes the bucket to the faucet, rinses it out, and brings back water for washing out the tomb. She keeps a colored brush behind the door. She has dyed red hair and no hat. She is younger than most of the others. She jokes with the cats. Two other women who have come with her, in hats, sit on a bench and wait. They all know many of the same words.

Beyond high walls, gray streets with movie houses in session, papers blowing past them in the light before rain in the afternoon. At the intersections of the avenues, army trucks are waiting for anyone. Going to other intersections. More trucks come in along the avenues, and stop, and let people off who were coming to a particular intersection, and other people, who were going away, get on. The green cloth sides of the trucks have been rolled up and tied. There are benches running from front to back, as in the old days. The passengers climb up steps and walk along the benches as though they were on stages, treading the boards, about to receive prizes, and some who are passing stop and watch. The passengers sit facing outward over the heads of the passers-by. Pairs of knees all along. They don't know the neighbors to right or left. Not a word. Umbrellas. They read papers, or stare at the glare of the avenues, keeping the faces out of focus, waiting, gazing past the new buildings innocent of life.

O N a mountain whose name had been forgotten, a shepherd found a book in a cave.

He had been gathering stones to make a wall across the cave mouth, when he found it. It was under the last stone of a pile in a corner of the cave. He had never seen a book before. He had never heard of such a thing. He was frightened and crept back a few steps toward the cave mouth, watching it.

He wanted to see whether it breathed. Whether it was a thing that breathed, and if it was, he wanted to see how long it could go without breathing. The first and second things he wanted to know.

He wanted to see whether it was really dead, or only pretending to be dead. He had seen animals pretending to be dead, looking like that but shaped differently, crouched together or coiled up underneath. He had seen men pretending to be dead, looking like that but shaped differently, lying there with weapons hidden under them. He had seen, worst of all, beings that looked like men, and even looked as though they were breathing, suddenly turn into stones or logs or shadows, and pretend to be dead, only to follow him later until he was unable to tell whether he was asleep or awake. But they too were shaped differently, like logs, or stones, or shadows. Even if it was alive, this was none of those things. It must be something else. So he wanted to see what it was.

Then he wanted to see whether it was a door. He had heard of doors, like doors into real houses, but doors into the floors of caves. This, if it was a door, was a door like an old lost garment of something, gone stiff now, and strange to everyone, smelling of unending darkness, and hostile to the infant present. It had been lying alone in the darkness too long, the only book.

If it was a door it was a door like food, lying in front of him, submissive but alien. It had a few rows of patterns pressed into it. Tracks.

He bent forward and put his ear to it and listened.

Things might be asleep in those tracks now. Those might be their beds. The things might be out now, hunting, and come back to their beds, and he would be there. There would be many of them. He had heard of them, small people.

Maybe not, though.

He had heard of boxes. He began to want to know whether the thing was a box. He had even seen boxes. He had heard that some of the boxes still in the world had been found in dark hiding-places, in caves. Some of them had had valuable things in them, and some had had terrible things in them, and death itself hiding under the lids. Against these last, he knew, no human weapons gave protection. But he pulled his staff closer. The sun was going down. There was no fire.

It was almost dark. He afraid to touch the thing now with his hand. He was afraid to touch it just before night. But he was afraid to leave it. But he wanted to send the dog to bring the sheep up to the cave. But he couldn't bring the sheep into the cave now, with the book there. But already he could hardly see it. But when he moved forward, his own shadow, which for some time had been nothing but a shapeless cloud of darkness, moved forward also and covered the book. But he heard the sheep rustling and coughing outside the cave, lambs crying, not near enough. But he listened for the dog. But he could not hear it. But he thought of the night coming. Outside, in that part of his mind, stars were walking forward toward night until their lights were visible, and they came on walking, and stopped in their places, and then night carried them toward the mountains.

He listened for the fox.

He listened for the wolf.

He heard the wind that came after sundown and then went away by itself.

Then he wanted to hear whether he heard breathing in the cave, that wasn't his own breathing.

But then it seemed to have stopped.

He was listening. He was watching the place where he had last seen the thing, trying to remember exactly what it looked like.

But he kept thinking of wolves. There was one wolf he had seen many times, and he wanted to know whether it was the same wolf every time. Wherever he was, it always came alone, just at evening. He had never seen it come. Each time he had looked up and it was there, watching somewhere to one side of him. Each time he had fixed his eyes on the wolf, kept them there, almost stopped breathing, only to see, some time later, that he was watching a wolf-shaped patch of darkness, from which the animal had gone. He thought now that he must still be watching the wolf.

When the first light came into the cave he could see nothing at all in front of him. Then he felt his cheeks. They were wet with tears. Then he saw the book, and without waiting he crossed the cave, and bent down, and touched the book, and made his hand stay there. He felt a small animal, a small lightning, run up his arm, but it was not painful. He moved his fingers over the tracks. Then he straightened and put the fingers of his left hand into the palm of his right hand, and folded the fingers of his right hand over them, to comfort them, to talk with them and ask them. With one hand in the other, that way, he went out of the cave and down the slope.

The sheep were scattered. When he called the dog, he felt the tracks stir in the fingertips of his left hand. They stirred every time he called the dog. When the dog came it seemed to be afraid of him.

When he had the sheep together again, and the dog watching them, up by the cave, he went in to the book, and with both hands lifted an edge. When the book fell open, he knelt to look at the tracks. Many animals seemed to have passed there and he did not know any of them. When he tried to lift again, pages turned and the tracks went on. He came to the empty pages at the end. He knocked to see whether the bottom page was hollow. He lifted it and the whole book came up and he carried it out into the sunlight.

After that his life changed.

He stared at the book for hours every day. He wrapped it carefully in his sack when he changed pastures. He began to be able to remember some of the tracks. He thought there was a secret in them that he would discover. He looked for them in the world and sometimes he saw them, but alone, or in a different order, so that he thought the others must have disappeared. He began to remember the order in which the tracks came on the pages, and some of their repetitions, some of the groups in which they travelled together, some of the companies in which some of the groups travelled.

He thought he was coming closer all the time to learning the secret in the book which was making the book change his life.

But the book had infected him with a new fear—of

losing it. He guarded it carefully. He avoided other
shepherds. They became suspicious of him. They spied
on him. They followed him. They saw the book. They
saw him open it, stare at it, kneel, staring at it. They
stole it from him. They killed his dog so that he would
not be able to follow them. They tried to kill him. He got
away at night. He went on until nobody knew his lan-
guage. He was beaten. Everything else was taken away
from him. He was found in a marketplace, begging. As
he sat there he tried to trace some of the lost tracks in
the dust, to remember them. He was seized. He was taken
away and tortured, while they kept asking him questions
he did not understand. The tortures were stopped and
an old man led him away to a tent and gave him food
and had him washed and dressed in clean clothes. The
next morning they set out, and he with them. They
travelled for days, into the mountains. Everything got
older. They came to ancient rocks, ancient trees, a huge
ruin. A man even older than the first one seemed to be
the king there.

They led him to understand, with gestures, that they
wanted him to trace the track, in the dust. The old king
came to watch him make the marks, and stared at them,
and asked the shepherd questions no word of which the
shepherd understood.

They tried to teach him their language so that he could
explain what the tracks meant, because the old king had
heard of writing. They tried to learn the shepherd's
language, in case the meaning of the tracks could be ex-
pressed only in his native tongue. They learned to trace
the tracks themselves, to be ready for the day when he
would be able to tell their meaning.

He showed them the tracks again, here and there in
the world, and he saw that they treated each other, after-
wards, with care and reverence. He never came to
understand their language, nor they his, but they listened

to him, they bowed to him, they followed him, they waited on him, they gave him a place next to the king, nodding to him as though he were a mute. And to please them he went on trying to remember more tracks, till the end of his days, forgetting even so, getting the order wrong, forgetting more and more, and supplying it as best he could, from mere habit.

But he never tried to tell them where the cave was. No one ever knew. No one even knew what mountain it was on.

M Y little friends, my trusting friends, my thin
friends, little ugly girls, both of you, with whom
I have been a child, it is forbidden here. It is forbidden
to be a child here, and see, we cannot leave. It is forbidden
to run here, and we have run, through the dark, empty,
echoing green halls. It is forbidden to laugh here and
we have laughed, in the empty rat world, as we ran.
Whatever is forbidden is funny. Where there were stairs
we ran on the empty stairs, the cement stairs guarded
with signs and posters, and our breath ran with us hand
in hand. Before long we had forgotten how it began,
and when we had met, and what day had been before us.
Such a long time we had not known each other! It was
already late. No one was looking. We started to run.

You followed me, both of you, and of course we are
lost. But when we discovered it we were still laughing,
in the last dark corridor. The doors were locked long
ago. We came down the last hall to the green wooden
stairs, above which the light was a little better, hoping
to get out. We ran up the wooden stairs to the last land-
ing, and stood, still laughing, at the top. We tried to
hold our breaths and listen. We heard our hearts. We put
our hands to each other's hearts. Someone was coming.

We heard him coming through the sound of our hearts.
There are no doors on the landing. Nothing but boxes.

We piled them up so that we could reach the dirty sky-lights full of wires, where we hoped to get out. But they would not open, they were locked, and he was coming.

At last we saw him, in his thick shoes and orange shirt. He is old, but strong. He had caught us. He hates us. His heart is a secret. He started up the ladder. We were still laughing. We saw his glasses, reflecting the skylights, dirty and thick, and his eyes watching us over the tops of them, as he came up the ladder slowly, hating us step by step as though he had known us and had been watching for us. I took hold of the top of the ladder and pushed it over backwards, and he fell.

But he is scrambling, putting it back. He will come up again for us, watching us over his glasses.

My little friends, how did it begin? Why did you follow me? Where did you come from? Who are your parents? You have stopped laughing, but you are still trusting, thin, ugly. Where were you hoping to go when you got out?

Listen, it will be all right. He will not take us any-where. I will go down the ladder and throw him off it again. Perhaps I will break his glasses, as though they were the skylights. I will take away his keys. Climb down behind me. Keep away from his hands. We will get out and throw the keys away. You will escape. And I will never be a child again.

As we begin to dig we find that we are not the first. For all our knowledge of history, we are surprised. Others have dug before us. Did they find it? Did they take it away? How did they hear it was there? Was it there? Was it ever there? Why? What was it, really? Is it still there? What happened to them?

And that, again, is history. Which leaves us in ignorance.

We continue to dig. No one has been before us tomorrow.

And we dig alone. The true present is a place where only one can stand, who is standing there for the first time.

The Secret

A CARPENTER and a woodpecker met in another world. No one in that sphere needed comfort or shelter; neither the worm nor the hunger for it was to be found there; and in any case there was no wood in that world, so the carpenter and the woodpecker had found themselves deprived of those callings which each had thought he could not live without. Each remembered his former life only a little more clearly than we remember ours, in this world. Each felt that he himself might be anyone, and was willing to learn. When they met, each thought there was something familiar about the other, and each bowed and tried to speak.

But at first their languages flew past each other without meeting, and the carpenter and woodpecker stood staring across the space between them without understanding what had happened.

"What did you do?" the carpenter asked. It was the only way he knew how to put the question, and he tried again. "What did you do, before?"

The expression in the bird's eyes did not change. Then the woodpecker, in what it remembered of its language, asked the carpenter the same question, but with no better success. However, with the loss of what they had thought of as their purposes, the sense of time and its urgency had left them too, and neither of them was in any hurry.

They repeated their questions over and over. At last, in its eagerness to comprehend, the bird began hopping on one foot, whereupon the carpenter remembered an ancient pain in his thumb, stuck his thumb into his mouth, and beamed at the bird, with eyes full of the delight of sudden understanding. They embraced each other.

They repeated their first lesson over and over, with growing excitement, taking turns at asking the question, dancing on one foot, sucking a thumb or a wing-feather.

A wind sprang up, and the woodpecker was moved and made signs to remind the carpenter of the sighing of leaves and the bending of big trees. The carpenter understood the woodpecker to be extolling the satisfaction of planing a piece of wood, and he danced around and around with his thumb in his mouth. In the sky there was a drift of mackerel cloud, and he pointed to it in order to go on and describe the grain of the wood emerging under his hands, and the woodpecker looked and remembered the patterns made by insects under the bark, and it danced on one foot, and they embraced each other.

They became close companions, and little by little, out of evocations of what each knew of the nature of wood, they contrived something which they used as a language. Everything they saw or heard found a place in it, and it became for them the key to a treeless world. They even invented what they thought of as a song in the new idiom. It was composed as much of hopping and stroking and head-beating as it was of syllables uttered with a voice, but the carpenter and the woodpecker went along singing it happily, lone sharers of a deepening secret.

PETER the Hermit woke in a cave above a cold valley. Rain. He was a hardier man than I am, though I profess to be hardier than I am. What did Peter the Hermit profess, hardy as he was? Sometimes he slept standing.

From soft spring meadows, from fishy streams and shade, and forests full of creatures before tapestries he called those who were born to all that round life, the oppressed and oppressors of that moment, maker and taker, and made them listen, after a long time, though at first they ignored him. Either their beasts were fat, and they themselves happy at table and in bed, and hoping to get richer. Yet fearing for what they had— fire, imminence of disease, suddenness of death, urgency of life to come—and at the same time bored and believing that there was something else. Or they were full of black bile, hacking and hewing at each other. Or both. He persisted in drawing their attentions to their own pain, joy, and hope. And linking what they dreaded to what they concealed.

When they came to him, he told the men to leave everything, the women to send the men away to set free a city that not one of them had ever seen, which had been theirs for a thousand years, and in which they would all live forever once they had died. He convinced them with their bad dreams, he invented visions of bliss which they did not want to deny were theirs. They followed him through deliberate sleep, not daring to wake, contriving new theories of possession, imagining new fortifications, carving a long wet red road for the ox-cart of knowledge, it is written, they who could not read.

Some came back and were buried at home, having seen the city.

Nobody knows much about him. You either believe or you don't. There is only the cave he is said to have slept in. Nobody called him Peter. Nobody woke him. He may never have slept at all.

By the Grain Elevators

THIS afternoon in rolling, partly wooded country, still green, though the summer is far gone. Here in the north they are still harvesting. All day yesterday the harvesters maneuvered like tanks across the grain fields, under dark heavy clouds, racing with the menace of rain. Sound of their throbbing echoing along hillsides, their clacking and rumbling, all for one species that numbers its days. Last night they harvested long after dark. I listened, imagining the nocturnal animals of the soil, with a light not of the sun dawning for them. And the animal heads of the wheat, being harvested in their sleep: a sudden blinding light, suddenly going out around their closed eyes. I thought of those who would eat the bread that was harvested at night, that night, in haste, late. I listened to the night harvest, the approaching and receding noises of machines in the dark, and the syllables of human shouting, woven across the nearer cries of owls, waking the magpies and crows, drowning out the crickets, and the cheeping of mice, among the roots. I watched the beams advancing slowly across the blackness. It came into my mind how suddenly my father had become an old man, wanting to be old. The wheat was green, then, and it was another year. Last night I honored the change better than at the time. We are taught not to grieve, but having felt it, I slept peacefully. I woke once and it was over. They had gone home from the unlit stubble, taking the grain. It must have been the dew that made them stop. The night was still.

Today they began again as soon as the sun had burned off the lower mists. The lines of the woods were dark on the hills and between the fields. A few cattle in the woods. Brick farmhouses, and little streams crossing pastures, reflecting crows and the low gray rushing sky.

A sign said "Ferry," and I took that road, not to cross, but to see the river. Ahead of me were trucks and trucks of grain, going north. They converged from side-roads, ahead and behind. Together with them I left the open fields and entered the woods. The road was narrow. Barbed wire was stretched among the trees, higher than someone could reach. The road drops steeply to the shore. Many of the trucks continue across the ferry. They sit in lines and wait, for hours. Few still go at all to the grain elevators built from fortifications of the last war. The year it was declared, for some time their fathers went right on, just the same, with the harvesting, through week after week of perfect golden autumn days, many of them with horses or oxen. Then there was only the day harvest.

The Fair

THE streets are changing color. Small, narrow streets curving to cling to the sides of hill after hill. I came up here hours ago. Walls along the streets painted white, ivory, blue. Faded. Gardens spilling over the tops, here and there. Cobbles and mud. Passing steep cross streets that drop straight from the mountain to the harbor, a long way below. Each one a cold, shadowy draft. Looking down through them, much of the city out of sight, every time. Behind the houses, and beyond hills.

Now it is evening and the colors of the streets are deepening. It is almost time for me to go and call the tall, dark young woman who came to bring something back, this morning, to the big house at the edge of the city, where I am staying as a guest. She is an old friend of the family. They left us together. I had something to mail. She brought me into town.

Under a stained glass roof projecting from the front of a blue grocery shop fortified with lettuces and egg-plants, a large, bald, overweight, dominating man in a translucent, starched white shirt, with rings on his fat fingers, is telling a small group of shorter men, in suits, with their hats tilted back, about something that happened at the Fair, in town. The International Industrial Fair. Big money, big money. He says what they say down there.

An older man, to whom they all listen with blank respect, returns to the subject of the British tent, which was put up today. He is flanked by men of his own age, sitting on produce boxes, in their Sunday clothes. He tells what a brilliant tent it is. Red and white stripes. He says it came in an Australian boat. He was a sailor, and he has been there. He tells them about Australia.

It was the British tent, the same one, that the young woman and I watched going up, as we walked through the Fair, before lunch. We stopped as the red and white mountain climbed itself, leaning, swaying, the stripes unrolling and straightening. New, bright pavilion. Shining white ropes. Inside, the pipe railings and scaffoldings newly painted white. There were Australians among the crew putting up the tent.

There was a brown tent like that, which I then remembered having seen once, that had disappeared in turn to reveal a baseball field that had not been there before.

I had seen that tent put up in a lot at the outskirts of the town where I was a child. I had been coming back from a short trip with my father, in the first car. A circus tent. My father had talked about carrying water for elephants, though there were none to be seen. Later, an ageing soprano tried to make a come-back, in a tent on that same lot. Her dressing room was a smaller tent inside the big one. She came out in her blond wig and stood behind a box of tulips whose petals were the shapes of her body, and sang about how she was alone.

One time when there was nothing on that lot but grass, we had driven past all together, and my mother was talking about peaches and apricots so that I imagined them growing among their leaves.

The city is full: hotels, restaurants, cafés. People have come from all over the world to the Fair. Turning down the next cross street, I see the group still standing in front of the grocery store, gesturing. Radios out of upper windows, instead of their voices. Advertisements for soft drinks, between bursts of music.

P OSSIBLY it occurs to others among us, from time to
time, and perhaps even to more than one of us at
the same time and within sight of each other, to look up,
for some reason afterwards as irrevocable as a dream,
from the gestures and entire labors that will never really
seem natural to us, now in our lifetimes, and remember
the queen as she was when we were there, rather than
as we have come to imagine her. Then instantly, for all
of our polishing of the handles with our palms, we may
feel, each of us separately, a roughness as though the
wood were unpeeled and our hands were back without
the callouses again. At such moments we seem to have
straightened too suddenly. We are dazzled. We are over-
come. We hope no one notices. What has betrayed us,
or what have we betrayed? The gestures from which we
look up belong to labors that we have chosen deliberately
and even wilfully, and apparently we had imagined that
our choice had put us beyond doubt or even surprise. But
when we came to choose those labors we were no longer
children, and childhood is the time to learn things so
that they become shapes of the growing body. Once
that is no longer possible we have entered upon age,
with its fragments. By the time we were old enough
to choose, we could not help but doubt.

The ways we perform our present labors are not even

the ways of our own country, for that matter. What we have learned that is of use here we have garnered from foreigners, illiterates whose names we can scarcely pronounce, watching them every day as though they were new, and picking up, with what appeared to be the essence of the actions, the local and personal idiosyncracies, rehearsing the combinations awkwardly, feeling foolish, but going on, having to get the job done before the end of its unpredictable season. Certainly they are not gestures that we were born to—whatever that means, and it is something that we have come to question more and more often, though this too only to ourselves. It is hard to think of anything in our childhoods preparing us for these actions, and yet it is always this adult that the child was busy making. It is true that in those days we had not met the queen. For some of us she was not yet born.

We look up, then, touched by some impulse that is indeed ours but which we do not recognize and cannot later retrace, from a labor upon which we are voluntarily engaged, and which we have undertaken in her name, though she is aware of it only distantly if at all. It is some work that we have learned to do in the course of doing it: our different awkwardnesses have settled into habits, we have ceased to pay attention to our imitating and have developed primitive variants, original mistakes and graces that in due course were repeated, and entered upon destinies of their own. And suddenly we are overtaken as by a chill, or a dizziness on standing up in the sun, by the strangeness and lateness, the improbability of each of our movements and of the whole enterprise. And in that moment of awareness of the alien nature of what we are doing, it seems that we cannot have begun it for the reason we imagined, but must be working for something else perhaps inadmissible and even unknowable. All at once how unlikely, how preposterous it seems that she could ever set foot (that foot like painted china) in these muddy paths, and spend her days among these raw fields beside the river of hard water yellowing its stones, these caked and matted animals, and these attempts to repeat the shapes of palaces in logs which we have hewn ourselves—all of them things that have come to seem beautiful to us.

Smitten by the oddity of our efforts, and face to face with the unlikelihood of her ever inhabiting the place that we imagine we are preparing for her, it is then that we glimpse her for a while as we knew her—and ourselves as we knew her—and remember how silly she sometimes seemed to us, how ordinary, to tell the truth, and how undignified; on occasion, how capricious and shallow; how ignorant her accent sounded in certain of the stone rooms, so that we tried to avoid her there. But also how we managed, in those days, to refer to such things among ourselves, and to laugh at them even though we had been brought up to regard the person of the sovereign as beyond reproach, like one of the elements. Now, of course, we scarcely dare credit such thoughts, even when we are alone. No, we accuse the sudden lucidity itself of being a disguised temptation to surrender, if only for a moment—a disloyalty to the entire undertaking and to the hope that was behind it, and in time we find ourselves examining that hope, also. But meanwhile we are here, and the winters come sooner than we remember, and there is no one to prepare for them but ourselves.

And yet those who came here first, and chose the place, were right. She will not be able to stay on where she is, where we were children. She will be forced to leave, even to give up everything. She will bring it upon herself, perhaps by those very frivolities that we have managed to escape at last, here, and—it seems—almost to forget. A place must be made ready for her, and its

preparation has become the abiding and cheerful purpose
of our lives. A place that she will have read about, but
in which we will have learned to survive. Some of us
brought our families—but it must be said that others,
even some of the founders, have gone back, in spite of
everything.

Most improbable of all, at moments, are the decora-
tions, which we have fashioned in the winters, without
experience or skill, from strange materials, but accord-
ing to her taste as we remember it, or after drawings
of objects that she is known to be fond of. Baskets of
flowers cut into the log walls, wooden wreaths pegged
to the cow barns. A set of carved steps painted with her
flower and her initials in a crown, which we plan to use
in the great throne room, when we have time to build it.

A Voyage

MANY times when I was a child we had driven
past the octagonal stone school building that
had not been used in my lifetime nor in my parents'
lifetime. It sat out in a field, by then, and the plow went
past the door, drawn first by huge white horses, then
by tractors, crossing the place where the path had been,
and the one where the privy had been, and crops of
wheat and corn grew, and rattled around it and were
harvested. Whenever we passed the building, it meant,
if it was on the right, that we were going to visit my
parents' relatives—but my mother had none. And if it
was on the left, that we were coming away from them
again. Each time, if we had been gone for a winter or
so, we would say we hoped it had not been torn down.

And there I stood inside it when both parents were
gone. It was larger than I had expected. Long rays of
the afternoon sun came through the narrow stone win-
dows. It was later in the afternoon than the children
would have stayed. There were shelves around the walls,
with nothing on them. The plaster had been an ivory
beige. Corinthian flutings, painted white, around the
windows.

As I stood inside, listening to the dry stalks in the
field, everything was looking past me. I felt a tall heavy
wave wash over me and go on to break somewhere else,

and then I was there without it, casting a shadow in the beam from the window, looking at the shelves, thinking of the alphabet, and through it.

Perhaps the building's proportions made it seem larger inside than it looked from outside. With the years it had sunk into the ground. The wooden floor was rotten in places. Abroad, in Europe, in France, I had seen an octagonal dovecote, somewhat larger across, and much higher. As high as a castle tower or a church belfry. Wagon spokes of rafters. The walls speckled with light, but most of the shaft in shadow, lined with thousands of square stone niches built into the masonry, and beside each opening a recess to the left, and another to the right, for the nests. A few wild pigeons flapped in the rafters and on the stone window grilles.

The light on the patches of plaster behind the shelves was also reflected from an angled bay of the central reading room of the British Museum, some years earlier, with the reference dictionaries of language after language arranged alphabetically around it. Coastline, horizon, zodiac. Except for the doors.

The small panes that remained intact were pearly. Like the tall slender octagonal glasses, from which some had once expected to drink *acquavit*, on that ship which the Swedes had launched to be the pride of the new navy they hoped to build. Many of those who sailed out on her had studied all through their childhoods, in uniform, for that moment. I think the Swedish rulers were hoping to challenge the English, as the Spaniards had done. To hold the Baltic, first—some such idea. They were years building that ship, but not a toast was ever drunk on board. There were many gun decks, many rows of gun ports, much gilding—since the vessel would be a flagship. Many statues of ancient gods, deities from languages no longer spoken by children, auspices made of wood. Golden carvings representing sea spirits and players of music clambered over the high curling stern, which was black, as I recall. The launching was a royal occasion. Someone would have been to Venice and seen a doge marry the Adriatic, and heard the music. What animals did they eat, that day, from the points of their knives? Every Swede can still tell you that they christened the giant ship-of-the-line the *Wasa,* which now means the same thing, to start with, in every language, as soon as it is known.

It sailed down the coast with all its flags flying, its band playing in answer to the band on shore, everyone in full dress uniform, officers and men lining the rails or aloft in the rigging or manning the guns at the open gun ports and looking through them at the sea rushing past, the light of the northern day reflected in the spray. Everyone on shore watching, waving, shouting. Puffs from the cannons on shore, then the sound of the royal salute reaching the ship many seconds later, across the water. The vessel rounding the headland under full sail, in the brisk wind, and all its guns answering the salute. And then, so suddenly that the watchers on shore rubbed their eyes, to which tears had not yet arrived, the great ship sinking with all hands. Perhaps the sea flooded the open gun ports. Nobody knows for certain how it happened.

After three centuries light returned to the wreck, swimming down to it with air-hoses, peering in. Everything was preserved by the water there, and by the mud, the darkness, the newness of the objects themselves, when they sank. It was said that everything was just as it had been—as though anyone knew.

The crowns of Sweden had changed heads many times. The schoolhouse was already standing empty.

A proposition was put forward to raise the wreck intact from the sea bottom, and the king approved and subscribed royal funds for the enterprise. It took years to lace a harness around the vessel, in the mud, and hoist it, with pneumatic equipment, inch by inch toward the ultra-modern sections of floating drydock, on the surface. There was a royal celebration on the day when the ship first broke the surface of the water, from below.

Meanwhile, samples had been brought up and examined in laboratories. A method of preserving them from the air of our age had been devised. It included, for many of the materials, a chemical treatment to embalm the tissues not only of wood but of fabrics: clothing—much of it never worn—and sails, rigging, wet flags. And it assumed the construction of a hangar: a vast hall built to house—as eventually it did—the whole of the *Wasa,* indoors, in a controlled, surprisingly warm, temperature, cradled in a delicate scaffold-work of beams, with jets of tepid sea water playing over it continuously to keep its moisture at a measured level, black hoses winding through it, lights inside the hull showing the dripping interiors, while a swirling cloud of steam rises constantly around it toward the translucent ceiling —the new surface. Replicas of the original misted octagonal glasses from the ship are sold at the door, packed for travelling. A raised decorative band runs around the nacreous sides, like scars of shelves. I could check the facts, but this is something I remember.

The Ship from Costa Rica

At the edge of the city of towers a narrow park
runs for a mile or so along the river. When I lived
nearby I would often walk there in the afternoons.
Bridges for pedestrians, bicycles and baby-carriages
cross the heavy traffic of the expressway at regular
intervals, and ramps descend from their river ends into
the park. Thin branches of slaty trees reach toward the
suspended slopes, surround them, and wait, always ex-
pecting something else. The park is bounded by a rail-
ing, a barrier of the utmost simplicity, next to the
expressway, within arm's reach of the hurtling traffic.
That railing is never touched, and is evenly wrapped
in smoke. The gutter outside it is never swept by any-
thing except the wind of the passing cars. Another rail-
ing follows the main pathway along the top of the river
wall. It has been bent, here and there, and broken, in
places. All the way along, the top has been worn smooth
by hands, so that it shines. After heavy rain, or a mid-
winter thaw, the scattered spots of rust never last for
more than a day. Leaning on the railing, one can look
straight down the dark masonry of the river wall:
granite blocks perpetually wet with the heave and slap
of the polished leaden water, and exhaling its leaden
smell. Wakes of tugs and barges unfurl up the dank
wall, and fall away, leaving their shadows on it, drying.

Coming and going, the tide clings to the wall.

Between passages of hands, gulls watch the water from the cold bright rail. It has an age of its own, a function of the lives that have touched it, slipped along it, held onto it. It is older than the ore it was made of. Its icy curve reflects dimly, in the manner of frozen surfaces. Objects loom and vanish there as amorphous shadows: drifting gulls, the vast bridge high overhead with trains flickering slowly across it and traffic on it creeping through the sky above the river—all are there, but only their watery motions, their changes, are distinguishable. The far shore itself is mirrored there: its smoking factories, gas tanks painted like checkerboards, warehouses and wharves, are reduced to an indistinct margin on the unworn outer edge of the iron. They merge into a horizon of solid rust.

There is a silence in the park that always seems sudden, because of the din that encloses it. Trucks and cars roar beside it, trains rumble and clatter above it, horns blow, sirens and the whistles of tugs howl and blast along it, compressors, drills, tear at it—it remains there, they miss it, one steps down into it. Yelping of dogs and shrieks of children drift through it like small kites, and float away. At each season it contains the others. It was midwinter when I stood by the railing and saw my father on the far side of the river.

He had emerged from a high office in a rusted factory near the bridge: an edifice of many storeys, each of a different size and shape from the others, like the superstructure of a ship. A sugar factory. I had often stood and stared across at it. At that distance the buildings appear to have only one side, with nothing behind it. But even from so far away I could recognize him.

He was wearing only a shirt, in spite of the cold north wind. A fresh yellow shirt, the color of lighted office windows before dark. And no tie. He looked fatter than when I had last seen him, but the shirt was loose, and the sleeves fluttered in the wind. He stood leaning on the balcony railing, looking down at a ship, moored below, that had been unloading there for several days, its bow higher every day. It came from Costa Rica. I could not see what was being unloaded from it. I waved, but I was not surprised that he did not see me. He was not even wearing his glasses. At that time he still had nine years to live.

I waved again. What was he doing in the sugar factory, hundreds of miles from where he had been born and was living? I considered that if I were to walk to the nearest ramp, and away from the river, many blocks, to the bridge approach, it would be dark long before I even came in sight of the factory again. As I watched, he turned and went back in, and at once I began to wonder whether I had seen him at all. Of course I said nothing about it. And of course I knew he was far away all the time. Letters came from my mother, as usual. All was well. When I thought it had been only the day before yesterday that I had seen him, I realized that it had been longer than that, and then I tried to remember whether it had been Wednesday or Thursday, and was startled to think that it might even have been the Saturday before, and then for a moment I could not remember what day "today" was. I had been back more than once, and had not seen him. Then one afternoon he came out again.

I had stopped—as I had done each time I had returned to the park, since I had first seen him—for a long look at the factory. The same ship was still unloading, the stern almost as high as the bow. I thought it strange that they should take so long about the unloading. I wondered about the expense, and whether the factory owned the wharf. That same flag from the tropics flapping day after day in the wintry afternoon light. As I watched, the same door opened, and he stepped out, in his shirt-sleeves again, and put his hands on the balcony railing and stood looking down at the ship. I thought, as I had the first time, that he looked younger than he did at home. That, then, was the way he looked at the sugar factory—a life he never mentioned, a life of ships, distances, cargoes, easy-going gazing from balconies, without noticing the cold—whereas at home, in the life in which I was used to seeing him, he set the thermostat in the upper eighties and complained of drafts. Rays of the winter sunset passing between the piers of the bridge fixed the ship and the factory and the balcony in salmon light. I waved to him, but he was watching the ship, and even if he had looked up and across the river, he would have had the sun in his eyes. He straightened up, rubbed his arms—whose softness had always depressed me—and turned to look down the river, for a moment, before going back into the office behind him.

Seeing him a second time did not remove my earlier doubts; it exacerbated them, and awoke new ones. I wondered whether the man I had seen had been there at all. I wondered what that meant—in any sense—and why I had seen him, and how I knew that he was my father. For I knew that he was my father. Who I knew was living hundreds of miles inland, at that moment. The sun went down. The black puddles were frozen under the bridge. Why did I think I had seen him?

The bright weather of the first lengthening days continued, and the next afternoon I walked onto the long bridge across the river. The ship was still there, riding high in the water, again reflecting the sunset. As I leaned over the bridge railing, which was not polished, and reflected nothing, he came out again, on the balcony below me, and looked down into the empty ship. I thought that I could have called to him, but I knew that the distance was deceptive, and the traffic on the bridge was roaring behind me. The day was milder than the one before, and without wind. The tide was rising. I watched him for a long time, waiting for him to look up, and he did, but not toward the part of the bridge where I was waving. And then he went in, and I walked on, farther across the river, until I stood over the factory and could see the back of it, the trucks in the courtyard on the landward side, the chutes to another building, the open warehouse doors, the streets beyond. I considered going all the way across the bridge, and into the factory, and inquiring—what? Asking for my father? By what name? Asking for the man on the balcony? About what? There I was, older than my father had been when I was born. I looked across the bridge, down river, at the navy yard. I recalled the way my father had used the term "navy yard"—a phrase evoking secret privileges, participation in some arcane freedom and authority, in another time. Yet I knew that the phrase, as he used it, did not refer to the place I could see, with its gray hulls tied in bundles, but to somewhere inexplicably different, vanished, on another coast, with two wars between. I had never been able to imagine him having anything to do with ships. When he had shown me, once, a photograph of himself and friends, on their ship, in the first war, he had had to point himself out to me: sitting cross-legged, grinning, in a knitted hat, on top of a big tube called a ventilator. What he said was their ship looked like part of a building: a floor. When he showed me the brown picture I thought someone else was speaking to me, from behind him.

The day after I had seen him from the bridge, the ship was gone. I knew that he was still in the factory, but he did not come out that afternoon. In the days that followed I found it hard to believe that I had ever seen him, and I never saw him there again, alive.

The Old Boat

WHEN I took you out, that day, in the old boat, I meant for it to show you something, and now I would not be able to tell you what that was. I wanted for you to see it, not merely because you did not come from the same place I did. But you did come from far away, after all, from another country, over much water, with your pale flame of hair. And I had come long before, in a smaller boat—but you already know that. To tell the truth I had forgotten that voyage. Was it really heroic? Was I? If so, I hope it did not show. The boat from the old family boathouse, which is almost never taken out any more. Think of the dangers of those other times. Think of the women with babies, women who would never again see anything in the same light. Think how I did not want to come. Think how cold I must have been, in the winter. Guess, if you will, at the terror of my fires, and the temptation to hate my life, the vacancy, long before you were born. But that was not what I wanted to show you.

One time my mother took me out to the island to see the Statue of Liberty. She thought it would show me something, and I thought so too, though how could I say a thing like that? It must have been ten o'clock in the morning, and I was wearing a dark beret; I was somewhere between four and seven. I was never afraid when I was with her.

As we approached the island we slowed down and
came into a harbor surrounded by stone walls. She had
taught me the word "approach." The boat with its white
beams turned to the right and then swung to the left
and ran aground with a heavy sigh. There was excitement
around us, and people rushed to the rail with cries and
exclamations, but my mother told me they were silly.
She showed me that we had run aground in soft black
mud. She informed me that we were a little early. She
took a calm, knowledgeable interest in this routine event
which seemed to surprise others. She took me to see our
shadow on the green water of the harbor, in which the
mud had been rolled up—by us. Our own mud. Outside
the shadow of the railing our shadows waved back at us
from the water, when we waved. Fine spokes of light
radiated from our shadows, as they did from the raised
hand of the statue, in pictures, which I remembered.
She showed me the gouge in the mud, where we had
run aground, as the captain often did when he was early,
because he was young. She pointed out places where
the boat had run aground before, as people should have
realized. The harbor had not been constructed with a
view to this boat's being able to turn around in it easily.
It was being enlarged, but until the new wharf was
finished sometimes the boat had to run aground. She had
taught me the word "tugboat" at an earlier time, and
the word "ramp." Later I was convinced that Venus
and the Statue of Liberty had both been taken from the
same model, and perhaps I was told that—it might even
have been during the visit to the statue. But that was
not what I wanted to show you, or wanted the boat to
show you.

It was something to do with the boat itself, and not
just with when and where it was taken. The curving
of the ribs, did you see: an ancient shape akin to the
waves, to the reflections of mountains, and to the courses

of heavenly bodies? I made them myself, once. A little hull to show myself something I could not afterwards explain, something that cannot be kept in a boathouse under cobwebs each with its map of a need. Well, we went out in the old boat. It was past the middle of the day, and in a place I remembered I ran aground, deliberately, as though I were young or early, and we left the boat there with the tide going out, so that it would stand on earth near its drying anchor while the sun went down—I showed you that, as we walked away from it. You saw the gold earth rising out of the water, and on it the gold boat where we had been. Someone knew and would come for it, on the dark tide. As when the Ark grounded on Ararat, a little before sunset, and in the morning there was only the world that no one had spoken for.

On the Map

I N a part of the country where my parents lived before
I was born the brick streets are wearing away. At
the foot of steep walks often iron railings remain. Be-
yond many of the railings, then as now, the river. Out
in the country, a few miles from there, the river was
green. Small fish of sunlight quivered in it without
moving. My father and mother went there on a Sunday
with church friends, and after eating they sat under
a tree at the edge of the water, and someone who knew
them came with a folding camera and they turned their
heads away.

The old one-room brick canal office, that harks back
to before the railroad, is closed now. It is a comfort to
see it still standing, unnoticed. A thin, white-haired
widower, in starched shirt-sleeves, collar and tie, looks
after it, to occupy the time. He was born next door and
has lived in that house all his life. The canal passes out
of town at a different level from the river, with the
railroad track on one side, under the glare of a pearly
sky that is redoubled in the polished surface. The canal
is a long white beam. Light hides in itself.

White stone steps descend from the brick sidewalk
to the water every block and a half as long as there are
the ends of gardens. Brick walls. Fences. Tall stalks lean
against each other, late in summer, on a Sunday, forming

seeds. In the next town there is still a central square. There used to be a market there—some sect. But it was closed, of course, on Sundays. A church, in the square, with a bell tower. They marked it on their map, which they kept.

After the railroad turns away, the canal enters deep woods. Out there is the old college where they once talked of sending me. The name is familiar, from the beginning. The quiet of the woods, and a spring coolness, even in the clearing that contains the one large building and the smaller ones beyond. Curtains blowing from upper windows. Archers in the dusk, young men and women in traditional white, hardly speaking, smiling, shooting in turn, one at a time, into targets under the far trees, and never missing, while the dew gathers on the grass. The sound of the bows.

Ten

T EN o'clock, and nothing here looks like night. Nor like evening. The white sky is as light as at four in the afternoon—some hushed, overcast afternoon in summer. Summer: a past, a time remembered, a season buried in the antipodes. I recall with surprise that this, in fact, is summer; this too: this glassy air empty of birds, this blank unmodulated hour, this lidless night. The old woman might have locked the enamel clock face, with a half turn or a whole turn, and taken away the hour hand. But what she locked was the windowed front door, some time after supper. It looked like one of the mores of a close-fisted region: locking the house in the afternoon, against the empty woods. Now they are all asleep. They have vanished. There is not a sound in the low wooden house. The white curtain over the glass of the door gathers the light from outside and gleams more intensely than any part of the sky. It breathes, when everything else is still. It goes on breathing, far from the sea, and out of sight of the moon. The old woman put the key on a ledge of varnished wood, in the hall, and before she had gone it had been lying in that position for centuries: it had been removed in one piece—ledge, varnish, dust and all—without disturbing so much as its shadow, into the museum of summer. I cannot hear whether the tall clock with the enamel face, standing in the hall near the key, is going or not. I put my ear to the wooden case varnished the same color as the ledge. Yes: far away a dry leaf rocking. But it is slow, according to the silent alarm clock in the next room, standing on a table piled with old magazines. Ten after ten, in there. Hanging on the wall, in that room papered with rusted vines, is a calendar ten years old turned to a month of spring, and a faded photograph of a field of daffodils, beside blue water, under a blue sky. At the foot of the calendar, a vase full of dusty plastic poppies.

The room on this side of the hall, the one that has been given to me—what was it before? It is hard to imagine that this building—squat, shapeless, a melting bungalow, on cement blocks, covered with green tar-paper shingles, some of them dog-eared and torn—ever had a dining room. But the walls were once conceived differently: the patterned wallpaper has been thinly painted over and still shows through the ivory brush-marks. The linoleum on the floor has been painted gray. A partition has been set up, near the wall farthest from the windows. What for? A shower that was never installed? And four iron cots have been arranged in a row, with their feet to the windows: half ward, half nursery.

She did not come from here, she told me. Not from this country at all. The language they speak here is not her native tongue. This was her husband's place, though not his house. This region, these woods. He had wanted to come back, talked of it for years, but had never returned. After he died, she had decided to come, by herself, to live away from the city. She spoke vaguely of sons, far away, with families of their own. The house in which her husband had been born and had spent his childhood had burned down, and the big barn with it. This house had been built afterwards, and the shack, half barn, half garage, facing it. Everything had run down, she told me. The people around here knew nothing. "Ignorant," she said, standing a little stooped, with folded arms, in an old cardigan, her head in a kerchief: the eternally foreign owner. A short heavy man with a white face that looked flattened against a glass, was splitting wood on a stump, beyond the house, in the gap in the elder bushes where the overgrown hedge opens into pasture, as she spoke. Chunk. Chunk. A sound coming across water. When I next looked he had disappeared: there was no one standing in the gap, in front of the glow from the pasture. Rusted hay-rakes, rotting wagons, the chassis of a truck—ancestors in daguerrotypes—emerge from the high green nettles and brambles. I saw them as I arrived: half-buried flotsam washed out into the woods. I see them through the white curtain on the door. I could take the key and go out. Nothing is moving out there. This lilacs have finished blooming. Along the one bend of a stream motionless willow bay is in flower. The birches have grown around and up through the stone foundation of the burned house that was a farm in another century, and they have overflowed the foundations of the barn: the dark walls are becoming transparent before the woods that are at once older and younger than they. On the side toward the house a cement loading ramp rises out of the mid-summer growth and leads up to a mossy platform surrounded by nettle and elder leaves. The pile of split firewood gleams at the foot of bushes as tall as the woods. There are no shadows out there.

It is the only farm (if it can still be called a farm) in the woods. And the woods—they are the horizon, from a long way off, and I went on beside them and they came closer. Other farms in the region stand far apart on the plain: red houses with ladders against them, floating in hay fields in the long gold evening, while the dust turns slowly to mist the color of the sky. They must be anchored, for they do not move. And they too are asleep in the shadowless light. Once I thought I would never see this hour. The farm then would be black on its hill, against the black sky, with hulking great Theo asleep in his one shirt, in a black room, behind bare glass the color of the night, and his mother, whom no one else ever saw except from a distance, asleep somewhere else in the unseen house sagging toward its foundations. But I never saw it at this hour. That was the summer when I was ten, and I believed that the night was dark and not allowed. Theo had a huge white horse, and in the daytime, when it had rained, he would let me walk behind it with him, holding the plow handles. Sometimes he took his hands clear off them, when the plow was running easy, and I could hold them where they shone. We seemed to have the wind with us both ways; the cool furrows glistened along the slope, and I smelled them, and the horse, and Theo's shirt. Flocks of shrill birds wheeled around us, brushing us with their shadows, until Theo undid the links, at the end of the field, and we left the plow where it stood, and walked to the barn, with the horse dragging the traces and their tails flicking over the ground, and I went home to supper, long before the yellow sun went down. The cold summer had turned, but the days were said to be long yet.

Out beyond the shining pile of kindling, in the pasture, a big white horse comes into sight. It sheds light like the curtain I watch it through. I think that it too may be transparent. I stand wondering how long it has lived, or could have lived. It moves slowly toward the house, never looking at it. It stops to gaze into the fresh firewood. It turns and comes through the high elder hedge, nibbling here and there at a tuft of green. It passes the shed, on which an old ladder is hanging, and stands still in the space between the buildings, blowing at the ground on which it casts no shadow. Then it turns and walks past the loading ramp and the foundations of the barn and the house, into the woods. Still gleaming, it passes out of sight among the trees, like the white sun. Again nothing is moving, nothing has changed. I could take the key, and open the door, and go out and see, and no one would hear me.

A Parcel

ONE day a package of implements arrives in the mail, from a house I had known in my childhood. Most things from that house have been lost by then, or are not wanted at the moment. These things that have arrived are still useful. A few knives and spoons. It is a surprise to see wood, such as handles, after it has been put away for so long. The wood appears to be smaller, paler, or lighter or heavier than the memory of it. The origin of none of the pieces of metal and wood is known by anybody, now. Some of them belonged to my parents. Some of those pieces they had inherited. Some others were souvenirs, but not of places where my parents had ever been.

Here, far from where I was born, after I have lived in many houses, the late spring flowers are opening toward the southeast, and I do not know where any of these things came from.

I helped to dry these spoons in that one house where we lived together. I hear the water running in that kitchen. The clink of the plates at the draining board. A parade of refrigerator doors. A footstep on the linoleum, that I recognize as my mother's. We have all dissolved. I see the light in the kitchen, the reflections on the painted walls. There were places then, the same ones as now, where the silver of the spoons had been worn away, at the base of the bowl and where the handle rested. It was already so when the things were Margie's. The insides of the bowls were already scratched, so that they gave back no reflection. But I could hold two of them up to my closed eyelids and look, as though I were looking through them.

Then I took them down and went on looking.

The Ford

SLIDES of his travels. I thought oh yes, and dismissed the enthusiasm in his voice, that clearly was begging for attention. The lights were on, so the slides were faint and translucent on the wall. Brought out in a hurry, with a touch of shyness, much of it false. There were other conversations going on. I listened here and there, for a moment, and so I missed the beginning of what he said about the pictures. I turned back to them only at the mention of the horses, the tone of the voices agreeing, saying, "There they are," and the slight pause that came after that, an intake of breath, a wave falling back.

Pale yellow wall, half dissolved by a diaphanous section of lit sky, some other time of day, maybe a winter noon, or summer in the far north, reflected in a surface that must be water, a water, a piece of shore beyond it, a river bank, so a river, part of a river, part of what could be seen of it from one spot, at one instant in the past. The wall gone from behind it. And there they were, the horses. A line of them, crossing from right to left, all bays—the slides were in color. There were nine or ten of the horses, in water almost to their bellies, and it looked as though there might be others behind, out of the picture. They had flat white cloths on their backs —blankets, or thin packs, it was impossible to say which, as everyone finally agreed after asking each other. He

194

knew no more than the rest of us did. The horses were following a larger bay, several lengths ahead of them, who looked like a stallion, and had nothing at all on his back. There were no lines, traces, ropes, harness. The horses were travelling by themselves. Even on the wall they appeared to be moving, like smoke.

He said that he had not seen them when he took the picture. They weren't there, he said. He didn't see them. It was only after he got back, and had the rolls developed by the same special laboratory he always used, where they did good work, professional. Somebody asked the address.

He said it wasn't until he brought them home to look at with the projector that he saw the horses. It wasn't anything like a double exposure. There they were, wading the river, the legs out of sight in the water. Just in that one picture. Of the river. The only one of the river. He had thought he was just taking a picture of the river. Not even the river—that same building, from across the river.

"I know that place," one person said. "I asked about it once. All they had to say around there was that it had been there a long time. But it must have been something else. At one time."

I had scarcely noticed the building, on higher ground, looking no bigger than a single haycock, in the distance, to the left, well above the water and the horses. And as I looked harder, to make it out, the slide changed, and I saw the landscape across the river, no water, no horses. The landscape into which the horses would have been about to pass: stubble fields and unmown straw-gold meadows curving uphill into dark green woods, and in a clearing near the top, the same building, a little nearer but still small and doubtful. A cluster of roofs, and in the center a round tower, all the walls painted the red of barns, but darker, an ox-blood, dry blood, color—though it may have been the light at that time of day, or the distance, or the exposure, that made it look that shade. The slide changed again, and showed the wooden tower, much closer, with small windows on each floor. One roof, butted against it on the left, was clearly a habitation. Another wing, of corrugated iron, had been tacked against the tower at an angle, and was covered with tin, that had rusted. The dark red paint was peeling. The top of the tower rose in a point, like a hat. Another slide, taken from closer still, showed only the upper story of the house, and the top part of the tower. The curving rows of small windows, in sight of which the horses would pass. The windows looked as though lights were about to appear in them.

"Somebody living there?" one of the spectators asked.

"That's as near as I went," the man who had taken the picture said.

"I don't think anybody was actually living in it when I was there," said the one who had told them he knew the place. "But that was a few years ago."

"I was just taking pictures of that building," the man at the projector said. "I still don't know what it is."

"Looks like a farm," one of them said.

"Maybe at one time," another answered. "But it's not being used as a farm. The grass is too high."

"I wanted to get one picture of it from across the river," the man at the projector said again, now that they would understand. "And I never saw—"

"You'll have to go back," somebody said.

But the man said nothing. And then they started talking about where the horses were going, and where they might have got to, by then.

Wagon

M ID-SUMMER, not far from the sea. North. Long evening, everything finished, houses closed, cobbled streets washed and empty. Echoes prowling. Shadows horizontal. Upstairs in the hat factory there is a stuffed pheasant with a broken neck, and a large model of a seventeenth century merchant vessel, with a light bulb behind green and red portholes, and a light switch that does not work. The stairs, the halls, parts of all the rooms and the bathroom, are piled with dusty hatboxes. Downstairs the doors are locked with polished locks. Everything smells of leather, felt, and pipe-smoke.

Starched white curtains on the windows. Full moon. It never really gets dark. The light bellies out on things. The facades in the unpeopled street remain white while turning green and blue in the moonlight. The white paint on the window frames gleams like teeth. Even with its colors, dawn at first looks duller than the moonlight. Nothing stirs in the street.

Well before the early sunrise there is a sound of distant thunder. It fades, and then is there again, nearer. It approaches. It becomes continuous. The rumble can be felt in the house. The street echoes. The doors and windows rattle. It is a cart, a wagon. Big iron-bound wheel-rims racketing, banging on the cobbles, rolling globes of the thunder sound ahead of them. Their roar is shot through, split, hacked and hacked by the massive slapping together of the load of heavy sawn planks far too long for the wagon, and waving down behind, trying to touch. Looming and flapping closer, more than ever like thunder. Closer than anyone would have believed it could come, beating down every other sound, shaking every wall and painting, setting the dust adrift, and then passing, with no one looking out to see whether it cast a shadow or who was driving. Going by, high as the second story windows, and beginning to recede, and fading away until at last the heart is louder and the day begins.

A Street of Day

I KNOW the morning is not over, from the way the light quavers on the face of the yellow brick apartment building across the street, and flows along the slack telephone wires above the far sidewalk. Sections of shadow, where the wires, as they swing, appear to cross, race back and forth between the poles, never touching them. The sections change shape, as the daylight changes. At breakfast they were long and liquid. Now they are drier, shorter, and they hurry. I have asked whether they are messages, and have been told that they are not. They are nothing. So they make no sounds. I know the sounds they do not make. Early in the morning, a violin bow on a saw. Then the sound of the breath of an animal running. While I watch, there are words passing through those wires. They are the messages. They can only be heard by the people they are going to. They know nothing of the racing shadows they pass through. Neither the mouths that are speaking nor the ears that are listening are aware of those shadows.

This is the view from the dining room. Most times of day it is a little dark in there, as though one had just come in from outside, because the shades are drawn on the upper halves of the windows, and the gauzy curtains film over the rest. It is lighter in the bay window, over the street, than in the depths of the room, but I have been told not to go too near the windows and be seen looking out. The dark oval table holds a reflection of window, a sleeve of a cloud. Once I walked under the table, and long afterwards I was told of having done it: a thing too dangerous to repeat.

Up the street to the right it is earlier. Where the sidewalk opposite passes a courtyard between garages with gates made of green-painted boards, topped with broken barbed wire, which have stood open for so long that now they will not close, and black dust dances tirelessly on the cement inside, it is the hour of coming home with the morning's shopping, pushing carriages, stopping to talk—one carriage facing one way and one the other. Past the corner with the butcher shop, out of sight of the dining room and into the next block, which is set back (for the street is wider there) several paces to the west, more of the morning is left. The children have been swallowed up in school: it has just happened, and a hush has filled the streets. The air is cool. There is still some blue in all the colors. The whole day lies ahead, with time enough for anything. A great space on all sides. It is the hour when aunts on visits take their walks. People are still buying morning papers at the tiny store in the middle of the block, and have not yet started buying ice cream or candy. And in the block beyond, where the street narrows again, breakfast is being eaten in the shingled houses, brick houses, stuccoed houses, upstairs as well as downstairs. That is the block on which something is always about to appear, like a streetcar arriving around the far corner.

But that far corner is not the beginning. The street continues straight on, rising out of itself, becoming visible —I have seen it happen. There are blocks that I forget each time until I see them again. They lie in the hours before the day has been claimed, as though they were not moving. And past them, in the twilight before dawn, at the edge of the darkness in which sirens wailed and the monastery burned into black silence, there is the big stone building like a barn or boat house, on the eastern side of the street, which I saw only once, and wonder whether it is still there. In that block the street runs close to the edge of the cliff, and behind the building I saw the seaport spread out far below in the first colorless hazy light, and the breathless polished river beyond the docks. The streets were empty and wet with dew—I could smell it. The huge doors of the building, giving onto the street, were wide open. Barn doors, firehouse doors: they had been folded back to expose a room bigger than a garage, almost as big as a church. I could see that it was not ordinarily disclosed to the gaze of passers-by, and that no one was expected in the street at that hour. The big room was darker than the sky outside; it was lit only by a few candles on tall silver-wrapped candlesticks. Near the doors there was a wagon with a bier on it. The body was draped in stiff white and gold ecclesiastical vestments, with a gold mitre on its head, and a long gold staff in its hands. The feet were toward the open doors. Over the body two young men in white brocade vestments, wearing gold birettas, were bending, one on each side, holding candlesticks, and arranging folds of the drapery. They looked up and saw me and appeared surprised. Then they went on with what they were doing, and I could see that to stay would be an intrusion. That seems a long time ago.

Going the other way, it is afternoon almost at once. An old wooden house, on the first corner, is lived in by some people who are never seen. Beyond it, picket fences. Tall bushes. Nodding flowers. A block of small brick houses with low black iron railings along the sidewalk, where children come back from school in groups, with their mothers, and go in for something to eat. In there it is nice, quiet, musty, and the sideboards are old women.

By the time one gets to the park, the day is growing late, as you can see by the way a ball drops from the air, and can hear from the echoes of voices playing tag, and of a rope striking the pavement. Urns at the tops of columns mark the way home to supper, in a cool breeze.

The street itself goes on, after the park, down the long viaduct, through the dusk, while the lights come on, and sounds of hymns drift from evening services. From the foot of the viaduct the street heads out through the night in the port, and comes to an end at the ferry barns, which are closed at that hour. The wide cobbled plaza in front of them is empty except for one car with its lights out and no one in it, parked at the foot of one of the ramps. All of the ramps have been closed with criss-cross iron gates. There are few lights around the plaza. The city to which the ferries go looks nearer than it does by day. But over there even now the stars are going out above tall buildings, the sky is growing pale, and it is already tomorrow.

THROUGH dusk on summer fields far from habitations a stone wind is heard rising through a cut in a hill. A long note and a short one.

The earth is still twilit after sundown at the time when the ray first appears, in high summer, bleaching the path ahead of it. Then the linked shadow full of lighted windows that sweep the fields making them darker, not reflecting them, follows.

Rows of lives are looking out of sound they no longer hear. They think it is night here, as they pass, with their minds in other places.

Sparked between hills, the windows are erased at their own speed. Then the sky is deeper, though there are no stars yet. And the rare crickets are clearer, as when the wind drops.

Every railroad station exists in a dream. There is no way to avoid that. Now we can even imagine the railroads themselves ceasing to exist. What will stand then where the stations are now? If there should be any people in those places by then, what would they dream, perhaps many storeys up in what is now air? They will not know that a station was ever there, the trains coming and going below them where they sleep. In a dream people still get on a familiar train, and the doors close, and they know where to look for the first field. When they see it, already the station is far behind, and each of them is in a different green afternoon.

BEFORE mid-summer I shake out my pockets in the sun. The trees pay no attention. The long grass is young green, full of buttercups. The unknown key, worn smooth in my pocket: it seldom sees the light yet it shines. I reproach myself, in passing, for indolence, lack of faith, not knowing the key. Leaves are shining pieces. When I look at them I feel myself trying to remember. But we are new.

Over the wall, bird-cherry trees, plum trees with green plums, oaks, an ivy thicket. Smell of bird-cherry, *prunus avium*. I can blame only myself for my age, and it is too late now to do anything about it. I feel responsible for what I have forgotten. Meanwhile, the sound of magpies, voices of stones in a river. I am words that I do not hear, but I grew up believing that I might. A photograph passes through three lives and the one in the middle never looks at it. In the flowering bird-cherry trees a flock of titmice have gathered for the first time of the year, as though it were already August. For the first time they make sounds that they were born knowing. The swallow and the goldfinch utter whole sentences of hard joy. How do I know? What is the first thing that I remember? It flew away.

Everything is flying. The sun is flying, and the trees; the living and the dead hand in hand. The jay flashes

through the intricate thickets like part of a storm, but
without crashing and without turning its head. It shrieks
for the victim, so that the victim hesitates. I try to im-
agine the woods as they appear between the jay's eyes.
The green dark woods unfolding through the head of a
jay, at great speed, to that one syllable, and no choice.
The needle jay.

The nightingale comes and sings in the shade of the
bird-cherry, too deep for the jay. I see only the woods
I can see. I am a foreigner, with this key. I watch. The
jay is preceded and followed by a brief hush such as
surrounds a wind skimming like a plate over the woods.
A taut, invisible horizon. Approaching it, the messenger
jay: *Change! Change!* When the echo has gone, the tit-
mice speak again, about August.

White-throat, black-cap. wren sing in turn in one
oak tree. As each of them sings a whole branch lights
up. The presence of singing. At moments the whole tree
lights up. The nightingale makes the whole tree light up,
in the middle of the day. Green light occurring as a sky-
lark makes morning. When the singing stops I go on
sitting with all that I remember, from there and from
many distances, and with all that I have forgotten, in that
grassy place in late Spring, after hearing something I
wanted to know.

THE rain drives from the west into the opening thistles. The finches: spools on nails, vehicles on spools.

An old affection for thistles. I hid once in a hollow behind a clump of thistles. They were surrounded by a thick bower of ferns, the summer's growth, green above, and rimmed and written on below, mingled with the sepias of other years in that place. It was evening in summer: few trees in the enormous rolling west light. Hummocks rising on all sides, full of rays: a flock of buffalo shining in their sleep. The thistles their constellation by day. We were all hiding behind the hummocks. In the hollows where we lay, the grass had been cropped by cows. We lay among the buffalo. The hollows were filled with shadow, which made them softer and deeper. Part of the shadow came from above, part from below. I became transparent. The thistles were my friends.

These are hare thistles. Where the hare comes, in the middle of the day, loping, sniffing, sitting and looking and looking, and then going on. When he leaves he does not know he is leaving, nor that I go with him part of the way.

Those were fern thistles. Ferns do not grow here, nor the smell, half-remembered, half-invented: chestnut, apple, pine.

These are rain thistles. They were not part of the game.

There are no hollows behind the thistles here. Limestone and sheep, mother and daughter, and the hare going on through the ages of colors, among the finch-wheels.

Beyond those thistles was the lake. When the hollows were full of shadow, voices would call us, from the shore, and we would all emerge, feeling the dew, and smiling at having won.

SWALLOWS glide hunting under the branches here, in the late afternoon. Rain flows east, when it comes. A dry ground most of the year, red, and shallow over stone. Every gray lives here, and changes like a cloud. The stones gather according to their kind. Waiting is here, no words, marjoram. Pink flowers of calamint, bees, seed-heads so small that a blade of tawny grass hides them. Straw is native, and the smell of heat, and cracked bark. The yellow thistles first opened to an evening in summer, and to them morning is always a surprise. The clipped sheep hurried past in the mist at sunrise, with dew on them full of light.

Mice flow out of crevices, shadows have rabbits, snakes leave their skins among the stones. At noon, underfoot, it is pure night, trembling with the same cicada sound as the day.

Long ago some human with an age came and thought to stay here, and decided where to put stones on top of each other, and which stones, and a roof over them. Nothing else is known of that person. Birth, name, face, death, friends. Above the stones there is the sky. In the summer, by the roofless house among oak trees, plums can be heard falling into the high grass a field away, hour after hour.

THE sea gleams all the way to the south horizon, on which there are two mountains, mirrors full of smoke. It is morning for all of us.

Lines of white foam are sliding in from the left hand. Breakers bright cerulean, and enamelled in some places. Curled porcelain, alive. Sun after ten days of storm. Large waves, green, suddenly shouldering out of riding swells, and running forward. In other places, slate of a long roof of breath passing inland. Invasions, ages, generations of bright foam proceeding at the same time over coral, to coral sand, after innumerable changes and distances, continue to arrive at no arrival at all.

Over the foam a haze of blown spray is rising and moving landward to join heavy clouds against the mountains of the coast, to the right, on the west: green ridges straight up and down, regular as statues, not statues of anything. Steep foothills marbled with red that is erosion, a skin parted and drawn back without a word. Valleys opening, filled, where they widen out, with palms and banana trees, foam of leaves. Valleys of sunbeams between dark cliffs. Rows of sharp buttresses, necks of stone horses running together, flecked with lichen. Water rushing in white falls between them. The word palisade has gone around the world, echoing.

Clear east, blue east, mother of loud unseen wind

without beginning, without name. Clouds gather on steep mountains, deepen, and their shadows blacken on dark, sharp, carved cliffs. They float through clefts. They fill high caves.

Two flat roofs, below, one on either side, hide parts of the sea. Neither roof is finished. A new tin chimney, on the one to the right, splashed with tar, is already turning the color of mist, a tower in our time. At the pace of the sea the rain is taking the mountains. Hammer sounds seem at first to be separate. Saw sounds run together. Rain disappears.

Harbor

RARELY is the night so clear, on this coast, at this time of year. All day we sailed in fog, floating through a pearl. The tide changed under us. We felt it, at times. The light went out of the pearl and we sailed on, through the back of a mirror, hearing the sound of a stream, which was ourselves, in the darkness. But we knew where we were, as one remembers parts of a story. We heard a buoy where it was supposed to be, and we passed it according to the instructions published for the season, which means us. Then suddenly the fog cleared, and we saw the night: many stars, and ahead of us and on either side an unbroken band of darkness. We were in the estuary. The sound of our passing through the water swallowed up the last low tones of the buoy behind us. Channel markers blinked, bells rang far off over the water as we made our way in.

We had not planned to arrive at night, but it makes no difference. I reach out over the stern and grasp the thick line that leads back to the patent log trailing behind us in the night to tell us our speed through the dark. I feel the pulsing of the line, the beat of the steady fish that is our time, and I reel in the heavy cord, hand over hand, stripping the water from it, hearing the metal fins break the surface and flounder over it until they come to hang upright, swinging in the night air, dripping into the babbling wake.

There are three of us: the old friend whose boat it is, the young woman whom he scarcely knows, who came with me, and I. After the long passage we speak little, sailing up the estuary, and when we do say something our voices are hushed and strained. We come to the end of a breakwater, where a small light is blinking on the top of a pole, and we turn into the stillness beyond it.

I remember the harbor in the evening, in another time: the glassy enclosure reflecting the cool sky full of yellow light after sunset and the one other vessel, a fishing boat moored alongside the looming fish canning factory—a structure like an old colliery, of wood and rusted tin, rising from the harbor's edge into the clear hour. One tall wharf. Ten or twelve houses around the shore; small, pointed white buildings from an age before any of us was born, with grass running down to the water, and some windows full of sky, some with drawn white curtains. Hydrangea bushes in the twilight, fading.

We move slowly across the still harbor. I can make out the tall black shape of the factory, and then the high wharf jutting toward us on its stilts. My old friend walks forward and we take down the sails and glide on, propelled by nothing but our own momentum, in a long curve that ends with the wharf a few feet away. I take a painter and wait until I see, moving slowly toward me, the black form of a long ladder. I reach out to it, and with the line coiled on my arm, start to climb. Step by step the pilings of the wharf sink under the stars.

We will hear our feet walk along the wharf and onto the echoing land, in the night. We will walk up the street between the few stores, past the speechless houses. Behind the curtains everyone is asleep. No one will know we are there. We will be standing in the street among the houses when the stars begin to fade, each of us seeing a different place. Unheard by us, someone will wake, on the other side of a curtain, and see us there, and not know who we are nor where we have come from.

W. S. Merwin

W. S. Merwin was born in New York City in 1927 and grew up in Union City, New Jersey, and in Scranton, Pennsylvania. From 1949 to 1951 he worked as a tutor in France, Portugal, and Majorca. After that, for several years he made the greater part of his living by translating from French, Spanish, Latin and Portuguese. Since 1954 several fellowships have been of great assistance. In addition to poetry, he has written articles, chiefly for *The Nation*, and radio scripts for the BBC. He has lived in Spain, England, France, Mexico and Hawaii, as well as New York City. His books of poetry are *A Mask for Janus* (1952), *The Dancing Bears* (1954), *Green with Beasts* (1956), *The Drunk in the Furnace* (1960), *The Moving Target* (1963), *The Lice* (1967), *The Carrier of Ladders* (1970), for which he was awarded the Pulitzer Prize, *Writings to an Unfinished Accompaniment* (1973), *The Compass Flower* (1977) and *Opening the Hand* (1983). His translations include *The Poem of the Cid* (1959), *Spanish Ballads* (1960), *The Satires of Persius* (1961), *Lazarillo de Tormes* (1962), *The Song of Roland* (1963), *Selected Translations 1948–1968* (1968), for which he won the P.E.N. Translation Prize for 1968, *Transparence of the World*, a translation of his selection of poems by Jean Follain (1969), *Osip Mandelstam, Selected Poems* (with Clarence Brown) (1974), *Selected Translations, 1968–1978* (1979), *From the Spanish Morning* (1984) and *Four French Plays* (1984). He has also published three books of prose, *The Miner's Pale Children* (1970), *Houses and Travellers* (1977) and *Unframed Originals* (1982). In 1974 he was awarded The Fellowship of the Academy of American Poets. In 1979 he was awarded the Bollingen Prize for Poetry.